KEEPING THE U.S. COMPUTER INDUSTRY COMPETITIVE: DEFINING THE AGENDA

A COLLOQUIUM REPORT BY

THE COMPUTER SCIENCE AND TECHNOLOGY BOARD

COMMISSION ON PHYSICAL SCIENCES, MATHEMATICS, AND RESOURCES

NATIONAL RESEARCH COUNCIL

NATIONAL ACADEMY PRESS
WASHINGTON, D.C. 1990

Support for this project was provided by the following organizations and agencies: Air Force Office of Scientific Research (Grant No. N00014-87-J-1110), Apple Computer, Inc., Control Data Corporation, Cray Research, Inc., the Defense Advanced Research Projects Agency (Grant No. N00014-87-J-1110), Digital Equipment Corporation, Hewlett Packard, IBM Corporation, the National Aeronautics and Space Administration (Grant No. CDA-860535), the National Science Foundation (Grant No. CDA-860535), and the Office of Naval Research (Grant No. N00014-87-J-1110).

Library of Congress Catalog Card No. 89-63507
International Standard Book Number 0-309-04176-7

COVER: *Flare,* by Benoit B. Mandelbrot, IBM Fellow, IBM T. J. Watson Research Center, and a Foreign Associate of the National Academy of Sciences. Image courtesy of ACM Siggraph with permission of Professor Mandelbrot.

Shown is a framed fragment of a generalized Mandelbrot set—a set of numbers that produce strikingly beautiful images of mathematical complexity that, as they are magnified, reveal yet more detailed, infinitely nonrepeating tendrils, whorls, and curlicues.

Like the Mandelbrot set, the U.S. computer sector when viewed from afar may seem relatively well defined; upon closer examination, however, the industry is revealed to consist of a myriad of complex and evolving interdependencies, driven by technology and subject to the ever-changing constraints of the global marketplace.

Available from:

National Academy Press
2101 Constitution Avenue, NW
Washington, DC 20418

S064

Printed in the United States of America

Preface

On May 23, 1989, the Computer Science and Technology Board sponsored a colloquium in Washington, D.C., on the competitiveness of computer-related industries. The colloquium attracted a standing-room-only group of invited executives, government officials, academic analysts, and journalists. Participants discussed the structure of computer-related industries, evolving patterns of competition in global markets, and the roles of industry and government in making the most of U.S. strengths in computer-related technologies and markets.

The colloquium was organized by a steering committee chaired by Samuel H. Fuller, vice president of research at Digital Equipment Corporation. Other members of the steering committee included Robert W. Lucky, executive director for research in the communications sciences division of AT&T Bell Laboratories, William J. Spencer, vice president of the corporate research group at Xerox Corporation, and Irving Wladawsky-Berger, vice president of the data systems division and general manager of the Kingston facility at IBM Corporation.

This report is a distillation of the far-ranging colloquium discussions. It has two goals. First, it strives to open a window into the richness of the U.S. computer sector, a collection of interrelated industries that is by and large poorly understood by those outside the computer field. Second, it seeks to illuminate the range and depth of the challenges facing the computer sector. The report is aimed, in particular, at policymakers, but it is also intended to be of interest to leaders in and students of the computer sector.

> Joseph F. Traub, *Chairman*
> Computer Science and
> Technology Board

Contents

Executive Summary

In May 1989, top executives from the U.S. computer sector, joined by university and industry researchers, met with governmental policymakers for a one-day colloquium in Washington, D.C., to define an agenda for keeping the U.S. computer industry competitive. Conducted under the auspices of the Computer Science and Technology Board of the National Research Council, the colloquium encompassed the full range of computer industries—hardware, software, and services and systems integration—that collectively constitute the computer sector.

From this broad representation emerged a strong consensus on one central theme: *Ensuring that the United States remains preeminent in computing at the beginning of the next century requires strategic commitment, leadership, and collective will that cannot be attained with a "business as usual" approach by industry or government.* This conclusion was based on discussion in five major areas.

MAINTAINING U.S. COMPETITIVENESS

Strategic Intent

What is good for one firm—even the leader—in computer-related industries may not be good for the industry in question or for the computer sector as a whole. The exodus of U.S. merchant semiconductor manufacturers from dynamic random access memory (DRAM) markets is a prime example of this problem, but others exist. Advances by foreign firms that have licensed new microprocessor technology developed by innovative, cash-strapped U.S. companies raise the question, How can the nation secure a greater share of the returns from technologies that originate within its borders? Colloquium participants frequently made appeals for strategic commitment on the part of individual firms. Some suggested, however, that lower costs for borrowing capital and other incentives will be needed to counter the financial resources of foreign investors shopping for U.S. technology and to encourage firms to evaluate the long-term impacts of short-term business decisions. Indecision can be costly; cooperative projects under way in other nations and the successes of foreign firms that have not been deterred by occasional setbacks clearly illustrate the value of strategic commitment.

Cooperation

Competing in global technology markets requires cooperation within and among firms and between industry, universities, and government. Joint research efforts (such as SEMATECH and the Microelectronics and Computer Technology Corporation) are only a part of what is needed, although they represent a good start. The magnitude of the investment and risk associated with emerging technologies, the need for worldwide technology and business development, and the importance of timely actions are among the factors behind the growing push for cooperation.

Cooperation has already contributed to U.S. successes in the computer field, and the nation should build on those successes. Government-university-industry collaboration underlies U.S. leadership in technologies ranging from networked computing to artificial intelligence and parallel computing, and its potential underscores the value of a continuing dialogue. Within the computer sector, the success of the systems integration industry with interfirm alliances may be a harbinger of the future for other computer-related industries.

Manufacturing

More and more computers and components will resemble consumer electronics goods, taking on a commodity-like character with both quality and price determining market success; firms that are successful in these large-volume markets will be those with superior product design, manufacturing efficiency, and product quality. If weaknesses in manufacturing and in the integration of research, development, and manufacturing are not corrected, computer hardware manufacturers could find themselves serving only specialty markets. Manufacturing strengths are essential for competing in the high-volume markets that fuel revenue and technology growth. Moreover, product quality is increasingly key to customer differentiation among types and varieties of hardware and software.

Erosion of the semiconductor-manufacturing segment of the computer hardware industry jeopardizes the health of the entire sector. The flagging fortunes of U.S. semiconductor producers will not be confined to the electronic components segment of the hardware industry, if present trends persist. Manufacturing capabilities and capacity must be developed to assure a major domestic supply of DRAM chips and to preserve adequate supplies of other key components. U.S. leadership in computers, software, and related services depends on timely and economical access to such key components. However, the dominance of a few integrated Asian firms in important semiconductor technologies vests these companies with the potential for cartel-like control over inputs essential to U.S. computer manufacturing. To maintain adequate access over the long term, even extreme measures, such as government subsidies, may have to be considered.

Technology Development and Transfer

Some standardization is essential, but the optimal level is not clear-cut—the issue is one of balance. Most colloquium participants called for standards to facilitate computer-to-computer communication and exchange of data. But standardizing operating systems and other elements was more controversial. According to several participants, standardizing operating systems could stifle creativity, lock technology at a primitive stage, and open the industry to imitator firms that compete on the basis of low manufacturing costs rather than innovation. According to the opposing view, it could instead ensure a base level of conformance onto which innovative firms could add their own specialized hardware and applications, and it could make sophisticated systems cheaper and easier to use and thereby increase the productivity of the nation as a whole.

Computer and other technologies are converging. Consumer electronics, business computer systems, communications systems, and other business equipment (e.g., copiers) increasingly rely on a common set of technologies and components. This convergence can convey advantages to manufacturers with relatively broad product lines or correspondingly broad partnerships.

Systems technology is a domestic strength. Software and systems integration businesses are strong, thanks to U.S. strengths in designing and implementing complex systems. Concentrating further effort in these areas would build on existing strengths.

Technology transfer was the key to many of today's commercial successes, but U.S. computer firms have frequently failed to realize the commercial benefits of research conducted in the United States. Successful technology transfer is difficult, even chaotic. Organizational impediments within firms often result in the most fruitful transfers occurring to and from the outside. Further opportunities for transfers from universities and federal laboratories are too often missed. In an environment characterized by rapid change, delay and missed opportunity can be crippling, if not fatal.

Small entrepreneurial firms may dominate the popular view of innovation in the computer sector, but many important innovations originally emerged from research at large firms. While large firms may not always run with their inventions, small firms too often fail to acquire the manufacturing, marketing, and other business capabilities necessary to sustain market leadership. The cult of the entrepreneur seems to be an American phenomenon, and its appropriateness for the future was called into question by colloquium participants. Japan's large integrated firms are establishing an increasingly impressive record of innovation to go along with their manufacturing prowess, and large firms dominate technology and market advances in Europe. How to maximize the strengths of large and small firms and harness those strengths together will be key to achieving a more cooperative, strategic posture in the computer sector.

Infrastructure and Education

Enhancing information infrastructure will benefit producers and users of computer technology. Computer networks with limited interconnection and cumbersome or costly access contribute to what many colloquium participants saw as a failure of the country to achieve much of the promise of computers. Several participants proposed building a national advanced-technology computing and communications network that would enable a variety of computer-based activities and resources, while fostering advances in hardware and software technologies that would benefit the computer sector. Acknowledging that this concept raises a number of implementation and policy questions, participants suggested that federal proposals for a national research and education network were a good place to start.

Ultimately, the growth of the U.S. computer sector depends on high-quality education and training programs. Colloquium participants returned frequently to the need for education to make computing a more integral part of many activities, to make the U.S. population more comfortable with and interested in computing, and to ensure that we in the United States have the talent to advance computer-related technology and its commercialization.

SETTING THE AGENDA

Each issue highlighted by this colloquium is complex, and each poses a host of implementation questions. The task of communicating what the problems are and why they are problems is itself difficult, as illustrated by the discussions that took place at the colloquium. The Computer Science and Technology Board intends to examine several of these issues in more detail, and it urges decisionmakers in the computer industry and in government and academia to continue the dialogue needed to resolve key problems of mutual concern.

1
Overview

Although the competitiveness of key industries—most notably, semiconductor manufacturing—has seriously declined, the computer sector as a whole retains much vitality. U.S. firms dominate the fastest growing, and perhaps most lucrative, markets for computer-related goods and services. For example, more than 60 percent of the world software market, totaling about $65 billion in 1989 and growing at an annual rate of about 25 percent, is controlled by U.S.-based suppliers.[1,2] Similarly, domestic enterprises and their overseas subsidiaries reap the majority of the global revenues earned for designing and integrating computer systems, a market whose annual value colloquium participants estimated to be between $25 billion and $40 billion. Finally, U.S. computer manufacturers are by far the world's largest producers of computing and peripheral equipment; in 1989 they earned approximately half of the $134 billion generated worldwide by the production of computer systems per se and perhaps 45 percent of the $300 billion in total global revenues when systems software, service, maintenance, and leasing are included.[3,4] This position reflects, among other things, U.S. strengths in relatively large and advanced-technology computers. Whether this nation retains a vigorous presence in computer-related technologies depends on how it responds to changing terms of competition in a global economy.

For the U.S. computer sector, the rapid rate of technological change and the direction of that change have been key determinants of its competitive position. Recognizing that technological leadership does not automatically transfer from one generation of products to the next, the U.S. computer industry has traditionally invested heavily in research and development. In a recent study of 897 firms in over 40 industries, computer manufacturers averaged the highest investment as a percent of sales (8.2 percent) for all industries except one, software, which as an industry invested an average of 13.3 percent of sales revenues into R&D activities.[5]

High rates of technological advance, a hallmark of computer manufacturing, "change the structure of the industry in spans of 10 years or so," explained colloquium participant Richard S. Rosenbloom, professor at Harvard University's Graduate School of Business Administration. And the commercial manifestations of the change often defy prediction. Underscoring his point, Rosenbloom noted that a major 1977 study on the future of the computer industry addressed the development of microprocessors and large-scale integration but did not anticipate the impact of personal computers.

Rapid rates of technological change in computer hardware have been used as a competitive advantage by U.S. computer makers. U.S. manufacturers of workstations, for example, have managed to stave off foreign competitors in the $6 billion market by rapidly incorporating the results of research into their products. According to the U.S. Department of Commerce, U.S. makers of "low-end" workstations can now develop and introduce new products in only six months, while "high-end" manufacturers have reduced this period to two years.[6] In so doing, U.S. firms have maintained a two-generation lead over Japanese firms vying in the workstation market.

If trends that are already well established in the computer-manufacturing base continue, however, much, if not all, of the U.S. computer sector may falter. Even such value-added activities as software development, system design and integration, and after-sale maintenance may be in jeopardy. "Falling behind in computer technology . . . ," said Lawrence G. Tesler, vice president of advanced technology at Apple Computer, Inc., "is a very serious issue. The country got very galvanized about the idea of falling behind in space exploration 30 years ago, and it's just as important today that we do not fall behind in computer technology." Yet, according to Tesler, "We are losing our lead in software . . . slowly."

Jeffrey M. Heller, senior vice president and head of the technical services group at Electronic Data Systems, explained that the individual industries are interdependent, and so their fates are linked. "Our business [services and systems integration]," Heller said, "cannot exist on a long-term basis successfully without a healthy domestic industry in both the hardware and software business."

Meanwhile, political and economic developments worldwide are shaping computer-related markets of tomorrow. In particular, with the integration of the European Economic Community in 1992, Western Europe, with a population of about 320 million, will surpass the United States as the world's largest market. Four decades ago, the U.S. market was eight times larger than the next biggest, providing the nation's manufacturers with a large "home audience" for their products. Numbering more than 240 million, American consumers still are an attractive market but have already shown an increasingly strong willingness to buy foreign-made goods. As a result, U.S. firms, no longer assured of dominance in domestic markets, must compete for sales at home and abroad.

GLOBALIZATION AND COMPETITIVENESS

"Technology is a fluid," said John Doyle, executive vice president for business and development at Hewlett Packard. "It will go anywhere that it is needed."

Most computer-related markets have been international from the outset, and this has influenced policymaking in other countries. By the early 1960s, the nation's infant computer industry was already active in foreign markets, earning about 25 percent of its total revenues from sales abroad.[7] The success of world leader IBM, in particular, was a major catalyst in the decisions of foreign governments to shepherd the development of their fledgling computer industries. In 1966, for example, Japan's Ministry of International Trade and Industry designated the growth of the domestic computer industry as the number one priority for future economic growth. Not coincidentally, U.S. computer makers' share of the Japanese market began to fall, a decline abetted by formal and informal trade barriers. In the 1960s, sales of IBM computer equipment accounted for about 40 percent of the Japanese market; today, IBM's share is less than 15 percent.[8] Starting in the late 1970s, the Japanese share of the U.S. market increased dramatically, and within a decade, the United States had a $4 billion deficit in computer trade with Japan.

Computers are perhaps the best and most tangible evidence of a world economy. Generally, machines "made in the United States" are made from components, subassemblies, and assemblies manufactured by many different domestic and foreign firms, including offshore subsidiaries of U.S.-based companies. In its most extreme form, this internationalization of the computer has resulted in entirely foreign-built machines that are sold under the label of an American company.

Several colloquium participants referred to cost advantages and other incentives motivating U.S.-headquartered firms to establish manufacturing and other operations overseas. "I'm told that, if I want to build a semiconductor fabricator," explained Patrick A. Toole, senior vice president and general manager of technology products at IBM Corporation, "I can get practically everything paid for in some countries, like Singapore. You can get long-term tax incentives, you can get training assistance, you can get them to pay for all the tools. . . . That is their national policy with regard to growing and engaging in an emerging industry."

Although embodying different mechanisms, policies associated with integration of the European Economic Community will achieve similar results, pointed out Gordon E. Moore, chairman of the board at Intel Corporation, a U.S. semiconductor manufacturer. In addition to eliminating national trade barriers between the 12 member countries, "Europe '92" will establish rules of origin and local content requirements that will require today's exporters of integrated circuits to build the devices in Europe. "Intel avoided for 20 years doing any manufacturing in Europe, because it [did] not make sense," Moore said. Now, the company has "two teams running all over the continent, looking for the place we ought to build our plants. We export over a half a billion dollars [of products] to Europe every year. We are going to add a half billion dollars to our trade deficit because of '1992.'"

"What we are looking at is not 'fortress Europe,' but 'magnet Europe,'" added Hewlett Packard's Doyle.

C. Gordon Bell, vice president for research and development at Stardent Computer, Inc., a U.S.-based, Japanese-financed manufacturer of workstations, suggested that superior manufacturing skills available in foreign nations also motivate offshore location of plants. "The bottom line—why we manufacture in Japan—is, we are trying to transfer manufacturing technology to the United States, and we want quality," Bell said.

Benefiting from the resources and support of overseas environments is neither automatic nor enduring. IBM's Toole noted, for example, that a company that subcontracts too much of its manufacturing to offshore plants "will soon lose the expertise to design and the ability to innovate, because it won't get the feedback it needs." There are strategic dangers as well. Toole said that an underlying motive of host countries is to acquire the technology, and, he added, "it is not long before a competitor has been developed." Moreover, the cost advantages of offshore manufacturing can be transitory. A strong dollar, local wage levels, and the absence of trade barriers are strong incentives for offshore manufacturing, according to Toole, but "none of these factors is within a company's control."

Nevertheless, most colloquium participants said they expected offshore assembly of computer hardware to increase. Similarly, U.S.-headquartered companies are expected to invest more in foreign R&D. According to preliminary figures from the National Science Foundation (NSF), U.S. firms invested $5 billion in overseas research facilities in 1987, up 6.4 percent from the previous year.[9] U.S. computer manufacturers appear to be among the leaders in this trend. For example, IBM has two of its four major research centers overseas, and Hewlett Packard's four-year-old Integrated Systems Center in Bristol, England, accounts for about a third of that firm's central research effort. William J. Spencer, vice president and head of the corporate research group at Xerox Corporation, described Hewlett Packard's move as an "example of a major company taking a strategic view in its R&D investment." At the European facility, Hewlett Packard can "take advantage of a large cadre of highly talented people and an ability to build—add local value to compete effectively in Europe," Spencer said.

Tapping foreign talent and technology is essential for firms that do business in international markets, and many companies see their investments in overseas R&D as a necessary ante for full acceptance in foreign markets, according to observers. These investments also help counter the so-called "not-invented-here syndrome," the parochial view that all innovations originate in the United States. "The post-World-War-II era, when it was just automatically assumed that the United States led the world in everything, is over," NSF Deputy Directory John H. Moore has said.[10] "We need to wake up to the fact that there's a lot of good work going on elsewhere in the world. And we need to appreciate that fact and take advantage of it."

Investments overseas are also expanding beyond research and manufacturing, integrating the operations of firms headquartered in the United States more completely into the fabric of foreign economies. As Toole of IBM explained, "It is very important for U.S. computer companies to establish and grow market share in all of the markets where their products have a value to prospective companies. In the computer industry, it is extremely difficult to survive for long in either a market niche or a single geographical area orientation."

What is perhaps confusing to outside observers is how these international linkages are blurring the traditional concept of a "U.S. firm." Is a firm with its headquarters in the United States but with most of its capital assets and employees overseas truly a U.S. company? How does that firm differ from a U.S.-located subsidiary of a foreign company? Obviously, the answers to these questions have important implications for federal policy and for business. Colloquium participants grappled with these questions, offering a variety of opinions of what constitutes a U.S. firm (see box). Despite the diversity of views, most agreed that for a company to be considered a U.S. firm, it must contribute to building capital and raising the standard of living in this nation. One way to define the U.S. benefit is the value added by capital, management, design, engineering, manufacturing, distribution, sales, or service functions performed by people from the United States. In a heavily interdependent set of worldwide industries, a given country's benefit is likely to be measured by the value added, which supports employees, taxes, infrastructure, reinvestment, and ultimately the standard of living.

COOPERATION

Colloquium participants repeatedly addressed the issue of cooperation—cooperation between firms and among universities, government, and industry. Cooperative efforts abroad clearly stimulated examination of cooperation, but there was a strong perception that emerging technological and market challenges are creating a new mandate for cooperation in this country.

"Japanese companies, in particular, have mastered the art of cooperating in order to compete," explained colloquium participant David J. Teece, professor

What is a U.S. Firm?
Answers from Colloquium Participants

A reasonable definition [of a U.S. firm] for many purposes would be one with significant U.S. ownership and a fair share of technology manufacturing and development in the United States.

[A U.S. firm is] one where the majority of the board, top management and owners take a U.S.-centered view of the welfare of the firm (whether it is multinational or not) and can be expected to consider the effects of their actions on the welfare of the United States first. It is clear we know what a foreign firm is since we keep Philips (Signetics) out of SEMATECH. U.S. firms are the others.

What is meant, will be meant, should be meant are all important questions. The current connotation of a U.S. firm is one that is incorporated in the United States and has a plurality of its business interest in the United States or one whose tax payments are significant to the United States. A suggestion: A U.S. firm is one that is important to U.S. society and contributes to the well-being of the United States.

A U.S. firm is a company incorporated and headquartered in the United States, which designs, builds, and sells computers on a worldwide basis. Company control is with U.S. nationals. Design is within the United States to exploit particular technology skills. Financing is increasingly likely to come from outside the United States given the large supply of "cheap" dollars. Manufacturing may be done outside the United States using manufacturing, manufacturing-engineering, and assembly skills and foreign capital.

U.S. computer companies (and other large companies) become increasingly "global" in their operation and development/manufacturing, even research efforts, in addition to their traditional worldwide marketing. I would call a company a "U.S. firm" as opposed to Japanese, or German, [for example,] if the majority of ownership is U.S. based and, thus, its profits contribute to building capital and the standard of living in this country.

Today's products and services are marbled with international involvement. A high-tech product may well be designed in London, the software developed in France, the parts fabricated in Taiwan and the entire product assembled in Torino for sale in the United States. Which is more German, for example—a Volkswagen produced in Rio, or a Ford made in Stuttgart? Is the Nobel Prize awarded to a pair of Swiss scientists working for an American company in Lucerne a source of pride for Switzerland, or for the United States? Or both? In today's global marketplace, ownership is often irrelevant as a factor in a company's success. What really matters are the kinds of contributions a firm can make to the localities where it resides.

[I]n the rapid internationalization of business it is also important to ask, "What is the United States?" It is a country almost entirely populated by people who came from around the world to better their life. With the coming decline in work force size and existing deficiencies in U.S. education, we should be encouraging immigration of educated people from all countries.

It is no longer meaningful to talk of U.S. firms. It may be somewhat more meaningful to talk of "U.S.-based firms," if their headquarters are located in the United States, and at least half of their business is conducted there. The fact that the classic distinctions between domestic and foreign firms has all but disappeared raises important policy questions. Policies that are aimed to help "U.S. firms" can no longer be easily implemented. Accordingly, it is probably necessary to think about policies in terms of their impact on U.S. economic activity, rather than on U.S. firms.

of business administration and director of the Center for Research on Management at the University of California, Berkeley. Teece continued, "There has been, and there remains, a recognition that by acting together, sometimes with government assistance—but without governmental barriers—Japanese firms can do better than they might by competing alone. U.S. firms must also recognize that cooperation can be used to catch up with competitors, stay ahead of competitors, and respond to foreign industrial policies."

Sometimes called "alliance capitalism," Japan's efforts have inspired cooperative projects in many nations, including the United States. Some observers, like Teece, would argue that Japan's success makes cooperation an almost mandatory condition for long-term survival in global markets. Two corollaries follow from this argument. First, U.S. firms and the federal government must monitor the progress of the growing number of cooperative R&D projects under way overseas. Second, the government must be vigilant about trade barriers and other protectionist measures that other nations may take to nurture the growth of their computer industries.

Many colloquium participants questioned whether some of the relatively recent foreign cooperative research efforts, such as Japan's Fifth-Generation Computer project, would translate into commercial successes for participating firms. "No doubt exists whatsoever regarding the seriousness behind these efforts," said Sam R. Willcoxon, president of AT&T business markets group. "Whether they're a challenge remains to be seen."[11]

Collective industrial research projects in the U.S. computer sector are a recent development. Their formation was shaped by widening recognition that the complexity, scale, and risk of advanced computer-related technologies increasingly demand more resources than individual firms, even market leaders, can afford. Industry representatives at the colloquium commented most on SEMATECH, the semiconductor-manufacturing technology consortium jointly funded by private industry and the Department of Defense. They expressed optimism, but they noted that it was premature to judge the performance of this and other cooperative efforts in the computer sector. Regarding such efforts in general, Gordon Bell of Stardent Computer noted that cooperative research projects attract and sustain scientific and engineering talent.

While joint R&D projects have a longer history in this country than is typically recognized, they represent only one realization of the cooperative links that must extend horizontally and vertically from individual firms, according to IBM's Toole. "We must improve cooperation at levels within companies—between functions such as marketing, manufacturing, development, and research," Toole said. Relationships must also be developed with suppliers, customers, and, "more importantly these days, competitors." Toole also extended his web of industrial cooperation to encompass universities and government agencies.

"With the fierce competition we face throughout the world, we can no longer cling to traditional . . . arms-length, business-as-usual dealings," Toole said. "We must find new ways and new areas in which to cooperate at all levels." The prospects for doing this may be poor; several speakers suggested that U.S. firms, grounded in the ideals of free enterprise and competition, still do not know how to cooperate.

STANDARDIZATION

Standardization, the process of specifying technical requirements for computer hardware, software, and networking, has emerged as a strategic competitive issue. The market-shaping power of standards in the computer sector was first demonstrated 25 years ago. In 1964, IBM firmly entrenched itself as the world's leading computer manufacturer by establishing its own internal standard for computer components and peripherals, which was showcased in its 360 System of compatible computers. Software developed for one computer model in the family would run on any other machine in the IBM product line. This compatibility assured IBM's customers that all of their computer equipment would perform in essentially the same manner and that their hardware and software would not become obsolete with the next series of new product introductions.

For IBM, standardization permitted the company to spread its R&D costs over a wide array of products that served a large-volume market. By virtue of IBM's large market share, the company's proprietary standard became the industry standard. But because IBM controlled the standard, it could make changes, making it difficult for competitors to overtake the industry leader.

Today, with the proliferation of computing equipment and applications, there is a well-accepted need to develop standards that attain at least a certain level of compatibility and connectivity among the machines of different manufacturers. Indeed, more than 1,000 standards pertaining to computer-related technology have either been adopted or are under consideration by national and international standards-setting bodies.[12]

Computer-related firms throughout the world are keenly interested in the development of these nonproprietary standards, with many trying to influence the outcome of the decisions. Some firms (e.g., Sun Microsystems), for example, seek to have their own standards adopted by the entire industry. But debate is not limited to specific standards; it surrounds the entire issue of standardization.

Colloquium participants also engaged in the debate. At issue is where to draw the line between necessary standardization and excessive standardization. Virtually all agreed that standards are necessary for data storage and exchange and for communication. Beyond that point—at the level of operating systems and hardware elements—the consensus deteriorated. The relevant issues will be discussed in greater detail in each of the following chapters; the costs and benefits from the manufacturer's perspective will be summarized only briefly here.

Standardization expands markets and lowers costs. Moreover, by providing users with a greater array of compatible machines from which to choose, it increases competition. On the negative side, standardization, particularly if it is done too early in a technology's evolution, can freeze the technology at a "primitive stage," said Apple Computer's Tesler. In addition, Tesler and others noted that standardization can eliminate innovation as a prerequisite for entry into computer markets, thus placing greater emphasis on high-volume, low-cost production—a strength of Asian competitors. It also places a premium on protecting the intellectual property embodied in whatever innovative elements are present. Adequate safeguards (e.g., patents or copyrights) must be maintained and enforced, especially internationally, to ensure that the innovator receives appropriate return on investment.[13]

Given the global push for standardization, all colloquium participants agreed, the issue cannot be ignored. U.S. firms, they said, must confront the question of what level of standardization is best, or they risk having the matter settled by the competition.

THE GOVERNMENT ROLE

Perhaps the biggest gap in cooperation to bridge is the one between government and industry. Here, too, the nature of the relationship remains to be defined, even though the need for more constructive links between the two has been emphasized in nearly every one of the numerous studies that have examined the flagging competitiveness of American industry.

Ironically, the U.S. computer sector is a creature of government-industry cooperation, motivated by a strategic interest, namely, national security. During and after World War II, the Department of Defense funded well over half of the research that resulted in the first electronic computers, and it supported much of the work that led to subsequent refinements and innovations that made the machines commercial products. As Kenneth Flamm has noted, only 4 of the 12 major U.S. producers of digital computers in 1956 exist today.[14] Yet the technical roots of many of today's firms, old and new, he writes, "can be traced to experience accumulated in the pioneering days of computing" when almost all R&D was sponsored by the nation's military services. A congressional committee estimated that in 1959, 85 percent of electronics R&D in the United States was funded by the federal government.[15] By 1986 federal support had slipped, accounting for less than 30 percent of the funding for U.S. electronics R&D.[16] More than half of IBM's R&D during the 1950s was conducted under government contract, and even after the commercialization of computers had begun, over a third was government-supported in 1963.[17]

The U.S. government's influence extends over many of the important technological developments in computer hardware and software, sometimes creating marketing niches effectively exploited by IBM's U.S.-based competitors. For example, time-sharing, a product of work supported by what is now known as the Defense Advanced Research Projects Agency, was a boon to the Digital Equipment Corporation, whose PDP-6 computer was the first commercially available machine to offer the feature. Today the federal government, primarily through the Department of Defense, continues to fund much of the basic research in computer science and engineering, such as studies of gallium arsenide and other nonsilicon semiconducting materials. Some of today's leading-edge computing technologies—among them, parallel processing and artificial intelligence—are outgrowths of military-supported projects. This situation reflects the strong dependence of U.S. national security on advanced technology.

Although the precedent of cooperation between the government and the computer sector was established long ago, and the government continues to fund basic research important to the sector, the relationship that has evolved is not commensurate with changing global conditions. Indeed, many colloquium speakers observed that the cornerstone of this relationship—military sponsorship of computer-related R&D—is much weaker than it was two or three decades ago, while at the same time it is not sufficiently complemented by civilian support.

"In the absence of a national appreciation of the developing computer role," said Alan J. Perlis, professor of computer science at Yale University, "the support by the military of computer development has been essential and far-sighted." Yet Perlis and others noted the divergence of the military's needs and interests—such as "radiation hardening" of electronic devices—from those of the marketplace. "There has been too little effect on our economy, our society, our industry, and our quality," Perlis said. Military sponsorship tends to channel "computer development in far too narrow a way and prevents our society from adequately exploiting its potential."

In addition, factors crucial to success in commercial markets are not often high priorities in the development of products for the military. "There is a problem with using military funding to drive the direction of computer innovation," said James H. Morris, professor of computer science at Carnegie Mellon University. "People who work on such projects are force-fed with money and never get a feeling for costs or markets."

Further skewing the government-industry relationship is the fragmented regulatory and policymaking structure of the federal government. In the executive branch, as many as 12 federal agencies help shape and carry out policies that influence the activities of firms in the U.S. computer sector. In Congress, 9 of the 13 appropriations subcommittees are involved in determining the research budget and specific allocations.[18] This fragmentation and the lack of a coherent perspective on the cumulative effect of actions taken by widely dispersed units within the federal bureaucracy pose serious obstacles to achieving the coordination and cooperation that colloquium participants, as well as the Council on Competitiveness and other groups, argue is needed.

"Those who are likely to be in a position to implement any remedies," said Robert M. White, president of the National Academy of Engineering, "are found in many different organizations spread across the federal government and private industry. They deal in relative isolation with many separate and relative issues whether in trade policy, tax policy, procurement policy, employment and training programs, [or] research support. Until there is a meaningful interaction, it will be difficult to fashion a nationally coherent or coordinated response to the challenge that is now facing the U.S. computer sector."

These factors may contribute to the perception, expressed by Xerox's Spencer, that "cooperation between government and industry [seems like] an unnatural act. It seems so difficult for us to do."

By contrast, broad-based cooperation between government and industry has been a boon to the computer sectors of other nations. "Foreign industrial policy is affecting the outcomes in American markets all the time," said Teece of the University of California, Berkeley. To assume that market and price mechanisms guide firms to pursue individual optima that result in a maximum benefit for the nation—an assumption that, Teece said, "informs public policy in this nation today"—is to ignore other important factors at work, including actions of foreign governments.

Some colloquium participants suggested that the nation has a government-directed industrial policy, in the form of a composite of fragmented decisions in areas ranging from defense spending and overall government procurement to antitrust laws. Moreover, several studies suggest that the success of strategically chosen industrial sectors in nations with such policies stems from factors other than direct government intervention.[19]

While it can be difficult to sort out the nature and impact of government actions in the United States as well as abroad, the computer sector must not be a passive observer in the policymaking process. Clyde V. Prestowitz, Jr., principal adviser on Japan affairs to the U.S. secretary of commerce from 1983 to 1986, said firms should be making greater efforts to present their views and suggestions to Congress and federal agencies. Patrick Toole of IBM noted, "We have to do it not only by meetings like this, but also by very strong industry associations."

"The main thing that makes the computer industry different from other industries is that the rapid change of the technology far exceeds the policymakers' ability to change," argued Heller of Electronic Data Systems. He suggested that this rigidity is the legacy of institutions shaped by concepts of law, education, work, and accounting that evolved during the industrial age. Cautioned Heller, "The heavily entrenched, industrial structural model works poorly in a service society and worse in an information-based world."

NOTES

1. U.S. Department of Commerce. "Computer Equipment and Software," *1989 U.S. Industrial Outlook* (Washington, D.C., 1989); 1989 world market estimate provided via personal communication from a Department of Commerce analyst.

2. Quantitative estimates within the computer sector are particularly sensitive to definitions and methodologies. Comparisons should be made with caution as different estimates seldom, if ever, measure the same market with the same methodology. The numbers used in this report are generally as reported by the Department of Commerce, supplemented where appropriate by industry and trade group data.

3. Gartner Group, Inc., Stamford, CT, 1989.

4. CBEMA. *Information Technology Industry Global Market Analysis,* Industry Marketing Statistics Committee, Washington, D.C., 1989.

5. *Business Week: Innovation in America,* October, 1989, pp. 177-228.

6. U.S. Department of Commerce, *1989 U.S. Industrial Outlook,* 1989, p. 26-11.

7. Flamm, Kenneth. *Creating the Computer* (Washington, D.C.: Brookings Institution, 1988), p. 101.

8. Dertouzos, Michael L., Richard K. Lester, and Robert M. Solow, MIT Commission on Industrial Productivity. *Made in America: Regaining the Productive Edge* (Cambridge, Mass.: MIT Press, 1989), pp. 262-263.

9. Buderi, Robert. "U.S. Companies Hike Investment in Foreign R&D," *The Scientist,* May 29, 1989, p. 1.

10. Buderi, *The Scientist,* 1989, pp. 1, 6.

11. One that bears watching, according to Stardent's Bell, is Japan's SIGMA project (see Chapter 3 of this report).

12. Gantz, John. "Standards: What they are. What they aren't," *Networking Management,* May, 1989, p. 23.

13. A Computer Science and Technology Board report on issues in the protection of intellectual property in software is anticipated in mid-1990.

14. Kenneth Flamm, *Creating the Computer,* 1988, p. 81.

15. Kenneth Flamm, *Creating the Computer,* 1988, p. 16.

16. American Electronics Association, 1989, as reported in *The Competitive Status of the U.S. Electronics Industry Sector,* U.S. Department of Commerce, 1989 (draft version).

17. American Electronics Association, in *The Competitive Status of the U.S. Electronics Industry Sector,* 1989, p. 94.

18. Council on Competitiveness. *Picking Up the Pace: The Commercial Challenge to American Innovation* (Washington, D.C., 1988).

19. "Even in Japan and France, countries where the state is reputed to shape the industrial structure in accordance with some national strategic vision," reported the MIT Commission on Industrial Productivity, "some of the most recent research is far more skeptical about the actual influence of state policy and more inclined to emphasize the role of private actors." (Dertouzos et al., *Made in America,* 1989, p. 109).

2
Hardware

The U.S. computer hardware industry, a diverse collection of small and large firms, is composed of three major and integrally related industries: semiconductor manufacturing equipment producers, semiconductor manufacturers, and manufacturers of computers ranging from personal and portable systems to supercomputers and associated peripheral equipment. The $4.6 billion U.S. semiconductor-manufacturing-equipment industry makes the tools—wafer-processing, testing, and assembly equipment—that semiconductor manufacturers use to fabricate integrated circuits and related electronic devices, the source of revenues totaling $24 billion in 1988.[1] In turn, 40 percent of all semiconductors sold in the United States are bought by domestic computer manufacturers, who, according to the Department of Commerce, were estimated to have sold $70 billion worth of computing equipment in 1989.[2] Perhaps double that amount may have been earned by domestic manufacturers in 1989 if systems software, service, maintenance, and leasing revenues are included, according to an industry trade group.[3] Each of these industries is, in turn, divided into segments defined by the products they make and sell. Colloquium participants did not systematically survey the hardware industry, but rather drew on their experiences to comment on what they saw as critical issues and trends.

Serious cracks have developed in the chainlike relationship between these important domestic industries. Weakest in the chain is the semiconductor industry, which at the start of this decade held commanding leads in world markets for virtually all types of integrated circuits. The Japanese pulled even with, and then surpassed, the approximately 250 U.S. merchant semiconductor manufacturers in percentage of world sales beginning in 1985. By 1988 Japanese manufacturers held a commanding 48 percent of the world market, whereas the world share for U.S. firms had fallen to 37 percent.[4]

Observers quoted in the media and at congressional hearings have described the decline as ruinous, and evidence from the domestic industries that are suppliers and clients of the U.S. semiconductor producers suggests that the description is apt. The position of the U.S. semiconductor-manufacturing-equipment industry has fallen precipitously relative to that of Japanese equipment makers. U.S. firms still claim more than half of the $7 billion world market, but their Japanese counterparts now lead in sales of lithography equipment (for imparting circuit designs on silicon wafers) and other critically important tools.[5] Some steps have been taken to arrest this decline, primarily through the formation of the SEMATECH consortium. More recently, several of the computer industry's leading hardware manufacturers have joined together in an ambitious effort to establish another major domestic supply of state-of-the-art dynamic random access memory (DRAM) chips. But this effort has only just begun, and its success is by no means certain. As it stands now, however, the nearly complete exit of U.S. merchant semiconductor suppliers from the market for DRAM chips—by far the world's largest market for semiconductors—weakens prospects for the equipment industry.

Computer manufacturers have felt the demise of U.S. DRAM production from the client end. Forced to buy the memory chips from Japanese producers, which account for 90 percent of the world DRAM market, most U.S. computer makers faced serious shortages in 1988. Some were forced to delay introductions of new products and to cut production.[6] Consumers also felt the pinch as rising DRAM prices translated into a 15 percent increase in the cost of some computer models. (IBM, which produces DRAM chips for use in its products, was less affected by the shortage.) In contrast, Japanese computer manufacturers, large integrated firms that produce semiconductors for their own diversified line of products and sell the rest on the world markets, avoided the bottleneck and continued to increase their relative share of international sales of computers.

The ripplelike effects and the contributing causes of what is now called the "DRAM fiasco" are instructive, and they will be discussed in greater detail below. Colloquium participants suggested that other segments of the hardware industry may experience comparable crises during the 1990s.

A comment by Gordon Moore of Intel, the U.S. firm that invented the DRAM but no longer makes the chip, underscores the gravity that many ascribe to the situation. "If you take the whole sequence of things," Moore said, "in the end we are all going to be dead, and the end may be nearer than we think because the whole structure necessary to remain competitive is, frankly, getting out of our control—increasingly."

SEMICONDUCTORS

Invented in the United States in 1959, the integrated circuit launched what many call the Computer Revolution, and a seemingly endless series of advances in device technology have sustained the revolution. Of the hundred-thousand-fold improvement in computer performance since the 1950s (measured as a function of the cost of information-processing capacity), the greatest share stems from innovations in component devices (e.g., central processing units and internal memory) built from integrated circuits. These devices are often referred to as "semiconductors," a reference to the base materials from which they are made.

For 20 years after the invention of the integrated circuit, U.S. firms' mastery of semiconductor technology translated into preeminence in world markets, and the rapidity of innovation was viewed as perpetuating the industry's dominance. In recent years, however, the relative importance of innovation as a competitive advantage has waned, and the value of manufacturing efficiency has risen, setting the stage for the U.S. industry's decline.

"[T]o a very great degree, the United States arena functions as a kind of public service organization for worldwide industry," said Charles Ferguson, postdoctoral associate at the Massachusetts Institute of Technology's Center for Technology Policy and Industrial Development. "We innovate and people thank us for the innovations that we develop and then incorporate them into their commercial products, which they then sell, often to us."

The "most spectacular and visible symptom" of this situation, according to Ferguson, is the nearly complete exodus of U.S. merchant semiconductor manufacturers (firms that produce electronic devices for sale to other companies) from DRAM markets. Indeed, Ferguson and many others at the colloquium suggested that this episode embodies the nature of the challenge confronting all of the interdependent segments of the hardware industry.

The "DRAM Fiasco"

Intel's Moore believes that Japan's rise in DRAM manufacturing began when the evolution of the technology shifted from a series of rapid, seemingly random advances to a predictable course. In the early 1970s, theory and practice demonstrated that memory capacity would quadruple about every three years, from 1 kilobit, to 4 kilobits, to 16 kilobits, and so on. Japan established a series of programs aimed at developing world-competitive capacity for manufacturing 64-kilobit DRAMs, but, aided by a booming market for memory chips during the late 1970s and early 1980s, that nation's firms beat the timetable. Japanese semiconductor manufacturers capitalized on the shortage to achieve a significant share of the market for 16-kilobit DRAMS.

"Beyond that," Moore said, "they went to their usual strategy of overinvestment," adding considerably to Japan's DRAM-manufacturing capacity. The firms then "engaged in dumping, selling significantly below their total cost," to sell the excess product that resulted from the overinvestment in capacity.

In the mid-1980s, demand for semiconductors dropped, triggering an industrywide recession and exacerbating the price-reducing effects of excess DRAM capacity. During that period, according to Moore, the Japanese firms demonstrated another attribute to go along with their manufacturing prowess—a "tremendous tolerance for pain."

During the DRAM glut of the mid-1980s, the Japanese industry lost an estimated $4 billion, about double the loss sustained by U.S. manufacturers. "Clearly, they won," Moore said. "They came out with a 90 percent market share in DRAMs, and we abandoned the business." According to MIT's Ferguson, "In 1986, the world DRAM market was $1.5 billion. This year [1989], it is probably going to be $10 billion"—approximately a sixfold increase.

Today the United States is home to three merchant manufacturers of DRAMs—Motorola, Micron Technologies, and Texas Instruments (which manufactures most of its components abroad)—and most observers believe the continued existence of the firms in this market is tenuous. With the exception of IBM, which has its own DRAM-manufacturing facility in Burlington, Vermont, U.S. computer makers are forced to shop overseas for much of their needed supply of memory chips.

Why did U.S. merchant semiconductor manufacturers choose to exit from the DRAM market? Moore's recounting of the factors underlying Intel's decision not to compete is illustrative.

By mid-1985, Intel had completed the design of a "good 1-megabit DRAM" and had worked out the manufacturing process, Moore said. Instead of proceeding to the mass-manufacturing stage, the company chose to forego making the $400 million investment in equipment required to compete for about a 10 percent share of the world market. According to Moore, the company could not afford the investment and decided to leave the market, opting to concentrate on logic circuits and erasable programmable read-only memories (EPROMs). "I think had we made the DRAM investment at that time," Moore said, "we would be a much weaker company today."

Today it is highly unlikely that an individual U.S. semiconductor firm would opt to enter the market and help bolster domestic production, according to Moore and others at the colloquium. In addition to Japan, South Korea and other Asian nations, as well as Western European countries, are building plants that will add greatly to world DRAM-manufacturing capacity.

"For a company to go into a business like that with the idea of making money," Moore said, "frankly seems like a real folly. It is going to require something more than the usual market motivations to get a significant reentry in the United States."

Free market economics would appear to suggest that the United States does not need to manufacture DRAMs, given that other countries appear to do so more cheaply and that the world semiconductor industry seems destined for another glut of memory chips. Computer makers and other customers can purchase their chips from overseas suppliers, and U.S. semiconductor producers can devote their resources to products with higher profit margins.

While acknowledging that this perspective is embodied in the tactical thinking of individual firms, many colloquium participants pointed out that the collective result of these tactical decisions can be sectorwide harm. The nearly complete loss of the DRAM market, they maintained, inflicted strategic damage on the entire hardware industry, and perhaps the entire U.S. computer sector.

Why? An answer is that DRAMs are technology drivers. Although their designs are far less sophisticated than those for logic devices, DRAMs have the densest circuitry of any integrated circuit: The same standard-cell unit may be repeated millions of times on a single chip. Thus DRAMs are the commercial test bed for tools and methods that achieve ever-finer line widths. Once perfected and mastered, this manufacturing technology allows chip makers to squeeze more and smaller transistors and other subcomponents onto their microprocessor chips, gate arrays, and other types of integrated circuits—the new devices that are the basis for the next round of improvements in computer equipment.

Consequently, in all but abandoning DRAM production, U.S. merchant semiconductor manufacturers lost the primary means for "addressing the kind of manufacturing issues that we have not done as well as the Japanese," Moore said. Moreover, the developers of the tools needed to correct these manufacturing weaknesses are suffering from the tandem effects of the loss of a major domestic market and the growing prowess of their competitors. Hewlett Packard's Doyle reported, for example, that a Japanese semiconductor company executive told him that 70 percent of the equipment in the firm's plant for making 1-megabit DRAMs had come from U.S. suppliers. In the company's facility for making the next generation of memory chips—4-megabit DRAMs—only 30 percent of the equipment had come from the United States.

"It is an extremely disturbing situation," said MIT's Ferguson. "If you are an American semiconductor producer, you have to ask yourself how deeply in your heart of hearts do you really trust Canon, Nikon, and Advantest. The answer cannot be terribly comforting." Nearly a quarter of Advantest, the world's largest maker of digital semiconductor test equipment, is owned by Fujitsu, a Japanese conglomerate that makes semiconductors, computers, and consumer electronics goods.

Even a company as large as IBM, which has a tradition of meeting many of its needs internally, is feeling the effects, finding that it must become more self-dependent than it might otherwise prefer. "We use the best of the U.S. infrastructure, which, unfortunately, is not enough," said Toole. "We have to supplement what is available in tools and materials by our own developments within the company."

The DRAM situation is emblematic of what many have characterized as the "hollowing out" of U.S. industry, the loss of the manufacturing infrastructure that supports many sectors of the economy.[7] The computer sector and the federal government have recognized this problem, and they have combined their resources to form the SEMATECH consortium, aimed at developing the advanced manufacturing technology needed for fabricating 4-megabit DRAMs and the next generation of logic circuits.

Even if SEMATECH meets all expectations, its success may not reinvigorate the semiconductor and semiconductor-manufacturing-equipment industries. In the area of DRAMs, for example, it is unlikely that an individual firm will take the risk and make the capital investment required to achieve a major presence in DRAM markets.

As a result, Moore and others said, the strategic commitment that building such a facility would require will not be forthcoming without external incentives or a means of distributing the inherent risk. Interestingly, shortly after the colloquium seven hardware manufacturers—Intel, IBM, Hewlett Packard, Digital Equipment Corporation, National Semiconductor, Advanced Micro Devices, and LSI Logic—announced their intention to build a joint manufacturing facility for producing memory chips. Called U.S. Memories, Inc., the facility would require about $1 billion in capital, half of it to be provided by the seven founding firms and by additional partner firms that are being sought. The rest would be raised through debt financing and other means. Although business details have not been made public, initial plans called for production of 4-megabit DRAMs—based on a design licensed from IBM—to begin in 1991. However, less than five months later, observers questioned the future of U.S. Memories after IBM announced it would license some 4-megabit DRAM technology to Micron and because of the absence of commitments by other major U.S. computer manufacturers.[8] While any one venture must be evaluated on its merits, these circumstances and the shadow they cast on U.S. Memories once again called into question U.S. industry's capacity for sustaining a strategic, cooperative effort.

Another means to help secure the still fragile position of U.S. semiconductor manufacturers, Moore and others noted, would be to subsidize memory-chip production to assure adequate supplies. Like federal subsidies for agricultural products, a DRAM subsidy would set a guaranteed minimum price for U.S.-made chips.

Beyond DRAMs

The U.S. semiconductor industry continues to maintain significant leads in microprocessors and other advanced areas of integrated circuit technology. In addition, colloquium participants predicted that the industry would continue to be the source of many of the innovations that drive the evolution of semiconductors and the products that use them, including computers. Participants were far less certain, however, about the marketing advantages that would convey with innovation, given the rapid diffusion of technology and the demonstrated manufacturing strengths of Japanese firms and other Asian nations.

"We had as big an advantage in DRAMs [as] we now have in microprocessors," said Moore. "I think it is a matter of time until the competition is just as strong there. We cannot keep moving to the edge and living there very effectively." Signs of this progression are already evident, particularly in markets for application-specific integrated circuits. DRAM-manufacturing capabilities are directly transferable to these fully or partially customized electronic devices, and Japanese firms now control about 40 percent of this high-growth market.[9]

Speeding the competition's catch-up efforts, according to several colloquium participants, are technology-licensing agreements that, while advantageous to individual firms, are strategically damaging to the hardware industry. Among the technologies transferred to Japanese semiconductor manufacturers in recent licensing agreements are two advanced microprocessor designs based on reduced instruction set computing (RISC) architecture. Licensing payments can alleviate individual firms' cash-flow problems, of particular concern to small start-up firms. Also, by accelerating the diffusion of a new technology, licensing can expand the relevant market. However, licensing can also work like a Trojan horse: Often, foreign licensees emerge as the top competitors in licensors' markets.

A particularly troubling aspect of the increase in licensing to foreign firms is that it reflects a relative dearth of licensing and other strategic alliances within the United States. Colloquium participants noted that large U.S. firms in the industry are often approached for financing from innovative start-up firms. But nearly as often, those large firms are not responsive, forcing the start-up company to look to the queue of foreign investors who come to the United States to shop for promising new technology developed by entrepreneurial companies. (See Chapter 5 for a discussion of this phenomenon.)

COMPUTER EQUIPMENT

Global competitive factors shaping the semiconductor industry are also influencing the world computer industry. Before the late 1970s, U.S. computer imports were virtually nonexistent; in 1988, sales of foreign-made computers and related equipment captured 39 percent of the $51 billion U.S. market.[10] As is the case for semiconductors, U.S. firms hold the dominant position in markets for technologically advanced products, such as supercomputers, superminicomputers, workstations, and high-performance machines with new processing architectures. But in the industry's largest unit-volume market, personal computers, foreign competitors account for more than 40 percent of worldwide sales, which are expected to total $25 billion in 1989.[11] Whether personal computers become the computer manufacturing industry's equivalent of the DRAM may well be determined by the manufacturing performance and strategic actions taken by U.S. firms during the 1990s.

The similarities between the competitive factors shaping the semiconductor and computer industries do not end there, however. The foremost foreign competitors in computer markets include many of the same Japanese firms that now account for more than about half of the worldwide sales of semiconductors. Not coincidentally, these firms have not experienced the same DRAM shortages that have beset many U.S. computer manufacturers.

"There is a great deal of evidence," said MIT's Ferguson, "that the memory market is subject to strategic control—whether coordinated or not is unclear. . . . It is subject to strategic control by the collection of vertically integrated Japanese electronics firms that dominate not only Japanese semiconductor production, but also Japanese computer, telecommunications equipment, and, to some extent, consumer electronics production. What is interesting about that, I think, is the striking degree to which this situation demonstrates the continuing ability of Japanese firms to both cooperate and compete." Similar trends are emerging among the growing computer sectors of other Asian countries, including Taiwan and South Korea, which are gaining a growing share of the personal computer market.

Like the pattern of competition facing U.S. semiconductor makers, the technological trends steering the evolution of the computer industry also are coming into view. These trends will promote significant changes in industry structure. Most significant, perhaps, is the commoditization of computers, particularly at the low end of the product spectrum.

Commoditization

Whereas individual companies may now manufacture thousands or several hundred thousands of machines in a year, soon the annual production levels of "each competitive, successful firm" will exceed millions of units, Ferguson predicted. "As a consequence, the ability to manufacture in very large volumes, the ability to design products rapidly, to insert them into production rapidly, to have a worldwide sourcing, manufacturing, and distribution network [will become] ever more important. That is an area in which . . . the United States is not doing very well."

C. Gordon Bell of Stardent Computer outlined the technological factors underlying this trend. According to Bell, all of the components that will be used in the commercially available machines in the year 2000 are now under development. His reading of the field suggests that personal computers at the start of the next century will be as powerful as today's supercomputers (while supercomputers of the day will themselves be far more powerful). Speeding this transition will be the already-visible movement to distributed computing environments, in which users can simultaneously exploit the resources and applications not only of their local machines but also of any number of computers that are accessible through a network. Both trends will increase demand for smaller computer systems, driving down their price and stimulating supply.

According to Bell, while the performance of all levels of computers (measured by the standard metric of millions of instructions per second, or MIPS) has been increasing at double-digit rates since the 1960s, the processing capabilities of microcomputers have been increasing at the astounding rate of about 40 percent annually, as compared with approximately 14 percent for minicomputers and mainframes. With the anticipated widespread use of RISC technology in microcomputers, performance of what traditionally has been the industry's low-end offerings will increase at an annual rate of 70 percent.

Bell did not foresee the extinction of high-end markets, such as for scientific uses and other computation-intensive tasks. But he raised questions about how demand for computers with different levels of performance will change. Will many people who require supercomputers today find that the powerful personal computers of tomorrow—operating alone or in combination with others—meet their needs? Will new applications and new approaches to problems emerge that cannot even be addressed with today's most powerful machines? Answers to these and other questions will determine the size, structure, and profitability of the computer industry in the future. Bell suggested that change will be relatively radical and that the vast majority of computers for sale at the beginning of the next century will resemble consumer electronics goods and will be produced in similar volumes.

Technological Convergence of Industries

The comparison of computers to consumer commodities was also made by Ferguson, who foresaw similarities that went beyond volumes of production. According to the MIT researcher, a common technology base of "digital optics, digital microelectronics, and digital magnetics"—the technology areas that have been the wellspring of advances in computer and telecommunications equipment—are "going to be used in a wide spectrum of products." Included in this category of products, by Ferguson's accounting, are digital facsimile machines, printers, high-definition televisions, and home communications and information systems. Early commercial versions of these items are already available; other products are under development.

An example of this new trend toward horizontal integration in design and production is Canon, a Japanese firm. Known to most American consumers as a manufacturer of cameras, Canon also makes laser printers, photocopiers, and photolithography equipment. With this diversification into new product lines, which exploit the same optical and electronic technologies, the company's revenues have increased tenfold—to $10 billion—during the last 10 years, Ferguson said.

While IBM has a broad product range, the U.S. computer-hardware industry overall is not characterized by extensive horizontal integration. Moreover, the virtually complete loss of the nation's consumer electronics industry makes it difficult for U.S. companies to exploit the converging technology base and the production economies of scope it implies and to diversify into many product lines.

Manufacturing

Both commoditization and convergence to a common technology base make manufacturing efficiency and flexibility essential for competing in domestic and global markets. "This scenario is manufacturing- and semiconductor-intense and, hence, subject to intense competition in areas in which we perform poorly," said Bell, adding later that the nation's general "lack of manufacturing ability" is the primary source of the hardware industry's declining competitiveness. According to Ferguson, "Industries already are making a transition to a mass-produced, low-unit-cost structure. Those industries are increasingly dominated by Asian firms."

Ferguson predicted that U.S. manufacturing weaknesses will become an increasingly costly liability as manufacturing capabilities become the primary "determinant of long-run competitive success" in computer manufacturing and the growing cluster of related industries. Moreover, the continuing—and, some would say, accelerating—erosion in the upstream industries that supply materials, manufacturing equipment, displays, and electronic components will handicap U.S. computer manufacturers' abilities to develop the necessary level of manufacturing proficiency.

"We have to find ways to improve and to protect our fragile manufacturing base," IBM's Toole said. "We are at a huge disadvantage because of the virtual absence of consumer electronics."

As pointed out in several studies, Japanese firms have achieved higher-quality products at lower cost through continuous improvement in processing. Incremental improvements, accomplished by fostering the translation of innovations into new products, can help a firm maintain a competitive advantage. A telling indicator of the different manufacturing perspectives of Japanese and American firms is their spending patterns. Citing a study by Edwin Mansfield, Doyle of Hewlett Packard noted that the average U.S. company spends 70 percent of its R&D budget on product development and only 30 percent on the manufacturing process. In the average Japanese firm, the percentages and priorities are reversed.

STANDARDIZATION

Hardly separate from the industry-shaping trends described above, the international push for standardization (affecting computer hardware, software, and data communications) is a catalyst in each hardware industry. Although carried out by domestic and international standards-setting bodies, the push is prompted by users seeking compatibility and interconnection among the machines of different manufacturers. Companies may also advocate standardization if a particular set of standards improves their competitive position or at least diminishes the advantages of the market leaders. Two examples, using IBM products, illustrate how standardization can be a boon or a bane to an individual company. Based on internally developed standards, the 360 System family of compatible computers cemented IBM's leadership position in the large international market for mainframes. The company's proprietary control of what became a de facto industry standard gave it a clear advantage, and other computer manufacturers directed their attention to market niches not filled by IBM mainframes.

IBM chose a different tack when it made its relatively late but hurried entry into the personal computer market, revealing its microcomputer architecture to the rest of the industry and purchasing the machine's operating system from an outside vendor. The openness of the company's standard was effective in promoting the development of software and peripherals by other firms, assuring, as IBM intended, that customers had ample support. The strategy made the IBM PC a marketing success. But within about five years after the computer was introduced, cheaper PC "clones," most assembled in the Far East, began to claim significant shares of the market, and they continue to do so. U.S. sales of imported clones in 1988 were up 50 percent over the previous year.[12] To confound clone manufacturers, IBM has introduced a new family of personal computers (the Personal System/2 series) with proprietary features.

While IBM was reasserting more proprietary control over its line of personal microcomputers, Sun Microsystems was exhibiting yet another approach to standardization, actively encouraging foreign and domestic firms to adopt its Sparc microprocessor. Some observers predict that Sun is destined to repeat IBM's experience with its personal computer, but Sun Chief Executive Scott McNealy espouses what others view as a pragmatic view of the drive for standardization. "I don't believe the world can go back to proprietary systems," McNealy said after his company licensed two Taiwanese firms to manufacture personal computers based on Sun's microprocessor design.[13] Sun is a staunch advocate of standardization, and through its licensing agreements with foreign and domestic firms, it is maneuvering to have its system adopted as the industry standard, thereby creating a relatively high-volume market.

Critics of the open-architecture stance taken by Sun and other U.S.-based companies argue that these firms have made it easier for foreign competitors to perfect the technology, speeding their entry into high-end computer markets now dominated by U.S. firms. Although colloquium participants did not agree on the point at which standardization handicaps innovation, most agreed that user demand for increased compatibility among the machines of different vendors and for a greater choice of applications will result in more hardware standards. Most also agreed that as the number of software and hardware features shared by different vendors increases, the importance of manufacturing efficiency increases, and more firms may enter computer markets, competing on the basis of cost and product quality rather than innovation. Given the nation's manufacturing weaknesses, IBM's Toole said, "Standardization will probably hurt both the technology and systems competitiveness of the United States, as it moves the contest to the area of Japan's greatest strengths."

NOTES

1. U.S. Department of Commerce. "Electronic Components, Equipment, and Semiconductors," *1989 U.S. Industrial Outlook* (Washington, D.C., 1989), p. 30-9; *1990 U.S. Industrial Outlook* (Washington, D.C., 1990).
2. U.S. Department of Commerce, *1990 U.S. Industrial Outlook,* 1990; figure provided via personal communication with a Department of Commerce analyst.
3. CBEMA. *Information Technology Industry Global Market Analysis,* Industry Marketing Statistics Committee, Washington, D.C., 1989.
4. Dataquest as cited in "Japanese Solidify Dominance of Semiconductor Market," *Washington Post,* January, 4, 1989, p. F1.
5. U.S. Department of Commerce. *1989 U.S. Industrial Outlook,* 1989, p. 30-9.
6. U.S. Department of Commerce. *1989 U.S. Industrial Outlook,* 1989, p. 26-2.
7. See, for example, Jodi T. Allen. "Regaining America's Dulled Industrial Edge: the Answer is Right Here at Home," *Washington Post,* May 10, 1989, p. F3.
8. Richards, Evelyn. "Future of Joint Chip Venture Now in Doubt," *Washington Post,* November 10, 1989, p. F1.
9. Dertouzos, Michael L., Richard K. Lester, and Robert M. Solow, MIT Commission on Industrial Productivity. *Made in America: Regaining the Productive Edge* (Cambridge, Mass.: MIT Press, 1989), p. 249.
10. U.S. Department of Commerce, *1989 U.S. Industrial Outlook,* 1989, p. 26-1.
11. U.S. Department of Commerce, *1989 U.S. Industrial Outlook,* 1989, pp. 26-9 to 26-11.
12. U.S. Department of Commerce, *1989 U.S. Industrial Outlook,* 1989, p. 26-7.
13. Fisher, Lawrence M. "2 Taiwan Licenses Set by Sun Microsystems," *New York Times,* June 22, 1989, p. D4.

3
Software

Growing at a rate of about 25 percent a year, estimated global revenues from sales of software exceeded $65 billion in 1989.[1] Moreover, when the value of software developed within businesses and other organizations is taken into account, the size of the market for software is much larger. Measured by salaries and other costs, the value of internally generated software in the United States may range between $150 billion and $200 billion.[2]

These figures are compelling evidence of the attractiveness of the software market, which is dominated by U.S. firms. They also attest to the increasingly important role that programs and their applications play in enhancing investments in hardware. Moreover, the growing emphasis on software development spurs the innovation of new equipment, which in turn creates ideas for new applications that require new software.

"As software gets developed," explained Alan Perlis of Yale University, "it exposes opportunities for the application and creation of hardware. The two work together, and there is no permanent boundary between them. There is a continuous shift, one way or another." Thus, for example, the emergence of new processing architectures, notably parallel processing, gives rise to a need for a whole new body of software—which may in turn enhance the development of new hardware.

The current situation has changed dramatically in less than 15 years. Prior to the introduction of the personal computer, software functioned somewhat as a "loss leader," an often-free inducement for buying—and continuing to buy—a particular vendor's computer equipment. Software development was part and parcel of hardware development, and computer manufacturers were nearly the sole source of programs, which were written to run on their machines only. The few independent software firms that did exist wrote programs tailored to individual vendor's machines. Sales of about a thousand copies were the benchmark for a highly successful software package.

Starting with Apple Computer's popularization of the personal computer, the size of the software market grew immensely, spawning small and large firms that derive all or most of their revenues from this market. Today a million copies of popular software packages may be sold. Moreover, increasing but still modest standardization has made it somewhat easier for developers to adapt programs for use on the computers of different manufacturers. In addition, even the largest computer companies recognize that they have neither the financial resources nor the technical staff necessary to provide the full array of software support that potential buyers of their machines now demand—while larger buyers of software, with similar resource limitations, look to the software industry to meet their needs affordably.

Out of these seeds grew the burgeoning software industry. Some U.S. software firms are now very large, the biggest reporting annual revenues of about $1 billion, but most are quite small, sometimes consisting of not much more than one or two people "with a personal computer and an idea." This diverse collection of U.S. firms accounts for more than 60 percent of world sales of software.[3] At present the U.S. industry enjoys a commanding lead in the world market, but hindsight suggests that no lead in markets for computers and computer-related parts is secure.

"Assuming some of the dire predictions . . . come true," said Samuel H. Fuller, vice president for research at the Digital Equipment Corporation, "then a large part of our hardware [will be] . . . manufactured and eventually designed outside the United States. Is there the kind of infrastructure and support in the other industries of the computer sector that they could remain, in fact, healthy industries in their own right? Can software exist as an industry without the supporting underlying hardware?" The answers to these questions are not clearcut, but Fuller suggested addressing potential problems before they become real ones. Software "is an area where we have to learn how to remain strong, rather than take it for granted," he said.

SOFTWARE: A HIGHLY UNUSUAL PRODUCT

Arguably one of the most important products of the age of high technology, software has properties that make it distinct from all other products. The largest and most sophisticated sets of programs, such as those written for air traffic control systems or early-warning defense systems, are among the most complex of human creations, rivaling the crowning physical achievements of modern engineering. Yet software development has features that make it more akin to an art or a craft than to a high-technology enterprise. It is an expensive, slow, and labor-intensive process that has undergone only incremental improvements in productivity.[4]

Another special characteristic of software is that it typically does not remain constant. Observed Perlis, "The thing that has been missed by software engineering to date, to everyone's great peril, is the concept of evolution—that software, as soon as it comes to exist, must change. The most successful software is that which is unstable and incomplete." Perlis explained that "unlike hardware, software gives the illusion that the costs of change are negligible since they apparently involve only scribblings. This is not so. Software affects its specification so that both undergo continuous change."

Other major properties that distinguish software, according to Perlis, are networking—toward the end of direct communication between programs, and automation—since "it must be the case that most of our programs run essentially independently of us." Finally, Perlis explained that "in the computer, programs are in a sense live. . . . They can do things we find extremely difficult to do—that is, to keep informed in a broad way about what is going on in the world."

Perhaps the most complex pieces of software entail integrating isolated collections of computer, communication, and other types of equipment into coherent information-processing systems. Systems-integration software, the means of accomplishing this complex linkage, often must be customized to meet the diverse requirements of customers, explained Laszlo A. Belady, vice president and program director for software research at Microelectronics and Computer Technology Corporation (MCC). Because of this customization process, software development can be considered as much a service activity as a manufacturing process.

Software is itself increasingly valuable in the production and modification of software. Researchers throughout the world are developing productivity-enhancing tools and methods for specifying, writing, editing, compiling, testing, and verifying programs. Although many are the proprietary possessions of individual companies, the tools already in hand have helped shorten the software development cycle, particularly for easily specified, straightforward applications. However, continued leadership in software calls for greater investments in developing and using software development tools. Noted Lawrence Tesler of Apple Computer, "In order to compete with, say, the Philippines where the labor costs are lower for programmers, we need to lower our overall cost of producing software by improving our tools."

In the software industry, low levels of productivity growth are a shared shortcoming, besetting firms in the United States, Japan, Western Europe, and everywhere else. In the United States, the most visible efforts to enhance productivity in software development, including the software research programs at MCC and the Software Productivity Consortium (SPC), were encouraged by frustrated users, notably defense contractors interested in reducing programming costs. The software industry has not pursued a coherent strategy to improve software development, not the least because of the implicit costs and uncertainties.

TOWARD A BIFURCATED MARKET

Current trends—in particular, the emergence of large-volume markets for packaged software and the growing demand for customized software—are stimulating a division within the industry, points out Laszlo Belady of MCC. One segment, he said, will concentrate on software packages that, although varying in size and complexity, can serve many different customers without major customized alterations. "These packages can be produced anywhere," said Belady, suggesting that U.S. firms serving this market will be most vulnerable to foreign competition because "everybody has the same chance."

In Belady's second category, systems integration, competition will be determined by the ability to manage complexity, to develop applications tailored to the idiosyncracies of individual enterprises: "What you have to do in order to make this complex integrated application work is to provide the glue, that is, additional software, which does the traffic control and holds the pieces together." This category, according to Belady, is where the greatest business opportunities may lie and where U.S. firms may have an inherent advantage.

Successful software of this second type can only be developed through extensive cooperation between the customer and the contractor, Belady emphasized, and "it is impossible to come up with a huge computerized integrated application for an enterprise where the vendor comes and does everything . . . it cannot be done without team work." For members of such teams, "it is not enough to teach programming," he said, "but you also have to give real-life experience, even at school, and teach people how to work together and not just to excel individually."

Belady explained that if we wish to master the necessary complexity of this second software category, we must exploit the potential of computers themselves in retraining individuals. He described retraining as "an incredible opportunity, an incredible benefit to the country." Belady stated that retraining could be invaluable in making this country more flexible and able to cope with the many new challenges that the "accelerating change of industry and society" confronts us with.

EDUCATION FOR BETTER SOFTWARE DEVELOPMENT AND USE

The link between education and the ability to stay competitive was made succinctly by Tesler: "If other countries have better-educated populations in computer science and software engineering, then we will fall behind." Many colloquium participants commented on the promise for improved education and training as means to achieve better software and better software development.

Colloquium participants cited university computer science programs as a particularly valuable asset to the software industry, because they provide needed personnel. "At times, people will argue that because of our education and because of our innovative spirit," observed Fuller, "we [the United States] will continue to hold a commanding lead in the area of software." The proportion of American-born students enrolled in these programs has dropped substantially, however. "Whereas it is bothersome that half of our graduate students are from foreign countries," said James H. Morris of Carnegie Mellon University, "we should try to make that a competitive advantage and give them every opportunity and encouragement to stay, both at the graduate and undergraduate level."

Getting the most out of software may, as Perlis suggested, entail developing systems that "get the human being out of the loop," but achieving that end requires human talent and skill. All colloquium participants had suggestions for improving educational programs in computer science and software engineering. Tesler, for example, pointed to the need for a practical perspective, commenting that "in terms of computer science and software education, what I would like to see coming from the colleges is people with more practical experience . . . [including experience doing] major projects on teams to revise other people's software, which is what one ends up doing in industry quite a lot." The value of increasing the exposure of faculty and graduate students to industrial software problems and development conditions has been noted elsewhere by the Computer Science and Technology Board.[5]

A recurring theme was the importance of interdisciplinary training that goes beyond software and hardware issues per se. Tesler related such training to maintaining a specific competitive advantage: "One thing that I think the United States can maintain a lead in is human interface design, which makes application software distinctive, but to do that, our students have to be very broad in their education. They cannot learn only technology; they have to learn something about psychology, something about art, and learning to work in teams with people of other disciplines. . . . We can stay ahead, particularly in the Far East, . . . by maintaining these cross-disciplinary development teams."

But participants' concerns about education extended to the general population. The health of the entire computer sector and the development of the technology will depend to a great degree on how society chooses to use computers and extend their applications. "The important thing to remember," said Yale's Perlis, "is that software is intended, as is the computer, . . . to make life more imaginative for all of us." He added that, because of the technology's influence, society will be changing continually.

Therefore, Perlis and others said, computing must be integrated into all areas of study. From growing familiarity with the technology among broad segments of the population, ideas for new applications will emerge, fostering the evolution of the technology and driving the growth of the software industry and others. "The effective use of computing," said Abraham Peled, vice president of systems research and director of computer sciences at IBM's T. J. Watson Research Center, "will be the key to the industrial competitiveness of the country as a whole, as products are conceived and developed inside a computer instead of the laboratory, and integrated directly with manufacturing [and] with the field force."

Education is an immediate concern. "If we see it as long-term, and therefore not requiring immediate attention, we will never get around to it," emphasized Tesler, "and I think that is what we have been doing in this country for the last 20 years."

FOREIGN CHALLENGE

Some erosion of the nation's lead in software markets is inevitable, but if limited, it could have positive effects, according to Apple Computer's Tesler. "Some degree of decline is healthy for the world economy," he said, and it will "stimulate more attention by U.S. software companies to international markets." Already, noted Tesler, "For routine types of software creation, the sorts of things that run businesses, . . . people are beginning to find that they can buy software development services from other countries ten times more cheaply than they can get them here." Several U.S. firms have already responded to this reality by establishing software development centers in such countries as Singapore and Ireland, where they benefit from relatively low labor costs. Domestic companies also "import" temporary foreign workers to write code for basic, or standard, software packages. India, for example, advocates exporting its programmers to work on international software conversion projects. How much of this activity takes place is not known, but it does involve leading U.S. companies.

Foreign production of packaged software is also growing. Tesler pointed out, "Some of the more innovative packages in the personal computer market have come from other countries, generally in Europe, say, France in particular. But as I have traveled around the world, I have seen interesting software in other places."

To enhance their competitive prospects, Japan and Western Europe have concentrated on developing productivity-enhancing tools and techniques, as well as methods for verifying the reliability of programs. To remedy gaps in expertise and to sidestep licensing restrictions, Japanese firms have also established software research laboratories in the United States. Other countries that have made their domestic software industries economic priorities, such as the People's Republic of China, India, Malaysia, and Taiwan, are focusing, for now, on large-volume reproduction of basic software rather than on innovation. Some firms in developing countries, capitalizing on the low cost of replicating software and weak international protection for intellectual property, market imitative packages.[6] Such copied products undercut sales of legitimate products and drain resources for legal action for copyright infringement.

The impacts of Japan's most visible efforts to achieve parity in software markets are uncertain. Colloquium participants saw neither the Japanese Fifth-Generation Computer project nor The Real-Time Operating System Nucleus (TRON) project as yielding breakthroughs that could threaten the U.S. software lead. They were more cautious in their appraisal of a cooperative effort involving government and industry to develop Software Industrialized Generator and Maintenance Aids (the SIGMA project). SIGMA "is a software production and industrialization system developed for the purpose of improving the fundamental environment for software development in Japan,"[7] building on AT&T's UNIX operating system. UNIX, developed by AT&T, is one of the leading candidates for a standardized computer operating system for the entire industry. The some 40 Japanese companies participating in the SIGMA project have all agreed to use a specific version of UNIX. With a standard operating system, according to one line of reasoning behind SIGMA, Japan could be able to address deficiencies in software development.

"The openness of UNIX," Morris of Carnegie Mellon warned, "makes it an ideal place for the Japanese to enter the U.S. software market. Look out."

While ongoing developments clearly indicate a Japanese push to penetrate U.S.-dominated software markets, these efforts may not pose the most formidable challenge to U.S. firms. "The real software competitor is Europe, not Japan," MCC's Belady maintained. "'Europe 1992' will reinforce the successes of [the cooperative research program] ESPRIT in the area of standardization and formal methods 'creeping' into industrial applications."[8]

The European Community has also emphasized development of so-called formal methods for software engineering. If successful, formal methods could make some software development more systematic and less craftlike. Moreover, formal methods can also enhance software quality by giving more assurance that software does not contain errors and will perform as specified.

Foreign competition has been constrained by U.S. dominance in computers, which has fed U.S. prominence in software. Although machine compatibility is increasing, getting the software developed for one vendor to work on the computers of another is far from effortless, and users are reluctant to switch to new hardware vendors and an associated new set of software vendors. Increasing standardization and, as has been the rule for three decades, continuing declines in the cost of hardware for a given level of performance could eliminate this barrier and open the door for increased foreign competition in software markets. Under these circumstances, it is imperative that U.S. software developers understand before their competition how to program computing structures that will emerge to achieve higher performance (e.g., multicomputers—distributed processing—and multiprocessors).

STANDARDIZATION

Software research in Europe and Japan has a common thread, a push toward standardization. Underlying this push is the undisputed assumption that standardization will improve productivity, lower the cost of software development, and increase competition. Virtually all software firms are advocates of these ends, but they disagree on whether standardization is the best means to achieve them. Discussions among colloquium participants were representative of this disagreement.

Comments by Apple's Tesler characterize one view of the issue. "Any standard that has to do with data communications—with exchange of data between computers—is absolutely critical," he said. He maintained that to standardize beyond that point would encourage competition from imitator firms and slow the rate of innovation in software and hardware.

"Standards and what goes on inside a computer are another matter," Tesler said. "Standardizing processor designs by standardizing operating systems, my company feels, [will make the] United States very vulnerable to competition from abroad. . . . Japan and [South] Korea do very well when they can find something that has been standardized, or [they] create a standard and then leverage that to reduce costs, reduce prices, and gain market share and take the market away."

Tesler continued, "One thing that we [at Apple] have done is very carefully protect the insides of our computer, both the operating systems software and the hardware designs, so that they cannot be copied. We are very bothered by the fact that there are moves in the industry to try to standardize on those sorts of things, because we think . . . that is basically giving away the show to the competition from the Far East."

Others in the industry are not bothered by the movement for a standardized operating system. As MCC's Belady noted, "Many people believe that standardization is necessary for progress." According to this view, standards establish a base level of conformance for well-developed technologies, freeing the industry to concentrate on areas where advances are likely to have a greater impact on the capabilities and applications of computers.

Raj Reddy, professor of computer science at Carnegie Mellon University, argued that failure to achieve some standardization of operating systems would be counterproductive, diluting the efforts of programmers, who are already in short supply, and draining financial resources. "I think we should be standardizing routine things, including operating systems, and trying to use our creativity at higher levels," Reddy said.

Preventing the adoption of standards is not the answer to maintaining competitive U.S. software and hardware industries, he maintained. If, in the future, foreign firms can produce powerful yet inexpensive workstations and U.S.

companies cannot, Reddy argued, the disparity will stem from a problem that is more fundamental than standardization.

The implications are similar for firms that develop software only. By fostering high levels of compatibility among the computers of different vendors, standardization would greatly expand software markets, uniting a fragmented customer base and eliminating the need to write unique code for each of the many operating systems that now exist. As for hardware manufacturers, efficiency of production would be a key determinant of the market success of software companies.

Fuller of DEC warned of a proliferation of standards and called for a more deliberate approach to the issue. "[W]ith too many standards, I believe, we will tie the hands of developers and inhibit innovation," he said. The challenge, as Fuller described it, is to develop a "set of well-selected standards" for hardware, software, and communication areas that are at a mature stage of technological evolution. "The rest of the playing field," areas where ideas and technology are changing rapidly, should be left "open for innovation," according to Fuller.

The questions of what to standardize and when to do it are as contentious as the issue of what the specifications for particular standards should be. Are operating systems at a mature stage of evolution, for example, or do significant advances lie ahead? Once in place, would standards make it difficult for new, superior ideas and technologies to gain acceptance and, ultimately, market share? Fuller suggested that effective standardization by many users on UNIX illustrates the mixed consequences of standardization.

Tesler noted, however, that reducing the cost of equipment is only one factor to be considered in decisions to develop or encourage standards. Noting that the cost-effectiveness of standards will decrease as they age and technology improves, Tesler said that companies that "leap ahead" of the standard will be excluded from a major segment of the market—the federal government and, perhaps, its contractors.

Debates over standardization will continue in domestic and international arenas. But if the push for standards continues to gain momentum, standardization will greatly influence the business strategies of software companies. Perhaps the only choice for U.S. firms, several speakers suggested, is to join forces and develop U.S. standards that are superior to those now under consideration.

"If the Japanese are getting together and making a standard," Reddy asked, "why do we not get together and make a better standard than they do, and always stay one step ahead of the competition?"

NOTES

1.   U.S. Department of Commerce. "Computer Equipment and Software," *1990 U.S. Industrial Outlook* (Washington, D.C., 1990); figure provided via personal communication with a Department of Commerce analyst.

2. Dertouzos, Michael L. Richard K. Lester, Robert M. Solow, MIT Commission on Industrial Productivity. *Made in America: Regaining the Productive Edge* (Cambridge, Mass.: MIT Press, 1989), p. 264.

3. U.S. Department of Commerce. "Computer Equipment and Software," *1989 U.S. Industrial Outlook* (Washington, D.C., 1989), p. 26-3.

4. Computer Science and Technology Board, National Research Council. *Scaling Up: A Research Agenda for Software Engineering,* (Washington, D.C.: National Academy Press, 1989).

5. Computer Science and Technology Board, *Scaling Up: A Research Agenda for Software Engineering,* 1989.

6. The CSTB has explored intellectual property issues in software through a workshop and forum in the fall of 1989. A report will be issued in mid-1990.

7. National Technical Information Service. "Foreign Technology," Abstract No. 37, 031, September 13, 1988.

8. ESPRIT, the European Strategic Program for Research and Development in Information Technology, is an umbrella program that encompasses some 200 specialized projects. One product that has emerged from ESPRIT is the Portable Common Tool Environment (PCTE), a standardized substrate, or foundation, for developing software for large systems. PCTE accommodates existing and emerging software engineering tools, which permits programmers to exchange tools and researchers to develop new ones that enhance the utility of the software substrate. Eureka, a European Community research and development program focused on commercially promising technologies and innovations, has provided funding for a software factory based on PCTE.

4

Services and Systems Integration

Once thought of as separate entities, telecommunications and computing equipment have merged to become "information technology," the umbrella term for the growing array of digital devices and software that gather, process, display, and exchange data and information. According to the Department of Commerce, revenues for computer professional services (e.g., contract programming, systems and network management, education and training on the use of computer systems) were expected to reach $37 billion in 1989.[1] The still-evolving merger of technologies has added emphasis to the notion that information is a strategic asset that every competitor must have. This notion has spawned a large and rapidly growing market for information-related services: database and videotext services, contract programming and design, value-added networks, training and education, data processing, systems integration, and others. Annual rates of growth in nearly all segments of the services industry exceed 10 percent; in some, growth rates top 20 percent and are expected to remain at that level for the near future.[2]

One booming segment, and potentially the most lucrative, is systems integration, which entails designing, implementing, and maintaining complex systems of computing and communication equipment and software, often in combination with other types of equipment and systems. Systems-integration firms help businesses and other clients achieve the desired interoperability of their information technology. The systems mesh technology—often a combination of equipment, software, and network-based services supplied by many different vendors—with an organization's activities, operations, structure, and planned development. Some firms specialize in turnkey systems, but most provide customized systems that are developed in accordance with customers' needs. In 1989, system integrators were expected to earn approximately $13 billion, with established firms reporting annual revenue increases of more than 15 percent in their domestic business and more than 25 percent in their foreign operations.[3]

Hardware and software manufacturers, accounting firms, communications companies, and other types of companies have targeted the systems-integration market, and the number of businesses diversifying into the market is growing rapidly. In 1988, more than 1,450 U.S. firms earned all or the bulk of their revenues from systems integration.[4] The U.S. market for systems integration is the world's largest, and it has attracted Western European and Japanese firms. Entry is achieved almost exclusively through acquisitions of U.S. firms rather than through start-up subsidiaries.

SYSTEMS INTEGRATION: A U.S. BUSINESS CONCEPT

The U.S. federal government launched systems integration in the 1960s, when federal agencies hired contracting firms to design large-scale systems to coordinate data processing or communication operations. Although still young and growing, the U.S. systems-integration industry is in a much more advanced stage of development than that of the emerging foreign competition. The difference, according to Jeffrey M. Heller of Electronic Data Systems (EDS), can be attributed to U.S. firms' early recognition of the business opportunities in integrating computing and communications equipment that organizations were assembling from various vendors as they tried to keep step with technological advances and the apparent opportunities they created. Building on expertise acquired in work done for the federal government, pioneering firms have recently branched into commercial markets, which were slow to develop at first but have been gaining momentum with the growth of private networks and other large-scale private applications.

"[T]he gradual move in the industry toward open systems architectures and networking standards," said Paul A. Turner, executive director of the Price Waterhouse Technology Center, "created an opportunity for brokers to interpose themselves between clients and the traditional proprietary hardware and software vendors."

For prospective clients, Turner added, systems-integration firms offered an "alluring" service: "a reduced tie-in to the proprietary systems of any one vendor, a more cost-effective solution to the needs of the client, made possible by 'cherry-picking' the best of the offerings of several vendors, and all this coupled with a single source of management and accountability that gave the chief information officer some degree of career insurance."

The attractiveness of the concept has been proven, compelling even vendors of hardware to set up systems-integration units that, in principle, are free to use the products of other manufacturers. Given the bright forecast for the industry, the stream of newcomers may increase.

"Systems integration," said Irving Wladawsky-Berger, vice president of IBM's data systems division and general manager of their Kingston facility, "is an area we all expect to continue to grow for a very simple reason: The same forces that are driving the technology and producing the tens of millions . . . of workstations with the networks and huge data bases, those same forces are driving complexity. This business would dry up if complexity disappeared, but I think there is about as good a chance of that happening as finding a parking space in Manhattan."

ELEMENTS OF SUCCESS

Being the first to market with a commercially valuable service is one obvious and important factor contributing to U.S. firms' dominance of the systems-integration market. Another is the large domestic market that served as a springboard for expansion into foreign markets, which are now growing more rapidly than the one in the United States.

Wladawsky-Berger and MCC's Belady suggested that an American flair for mastering complexity may also be fundamental to the strong showing of U.S. systems-integration firms. "Management of complexity is a most American endeavor; it really plays well to the things we are good at," Wladawsky-Berger said, summarizing the position thus: "It is skills intensive; it is highly technical and, so, our R&D effort will serve us well."

Turner of Price Waterhouse elaborated on the implications for skills. "As often happens," he said, "the major advances come from effort in those areas that fall between the cracks of the conventional disciplines. The skills . . . necessary to perform a radical reevaluation of system functionality include the conventional technical-system skills, but also vital are the skills needed to understand the business, [its] management, and the organizational issues. And also required, critically, is a problem-solving process that gets the people involved—and that is all of them, both users and systems designers, thinking outside the box and beyond the obvious solutions."

Inherent in the process of integrating multivendor information technology is the need to form flexible partnerships, not unlike the horizontal and vertical cooperative relationships that many have advocated for other industries in the computer sector. In the European market, for example, EDS competes "rather heavily at times with IBM," Heller explained. However, he noted, "we team together sometimes and [EDS is] their customer and they are ours. So, we have complex relationships."

"Seldom does a system integrator have all the resources needed to do a particular job," Turner added, "and these partnerships increasingly cross national boundaries and lead to a very complex set of interdependencies, but ones that are required in order to cope with the diversity and complexity of technology . . . ."

Other factors that underlie the success of U.S. systems-integration firms are neither unique to this market nor cultural in origin. Rather they are good business practices, sometimes applied in ways that may go beyond conventional expectations. Foremost among these is the demonstrated importance of developing close working relationships with customers, a point made by all industry representatives at the colloquium. Customers want, according to one speaker, a "total applications solution," requiring intricate understanding of a client's operations.

Price Waterhouse's Turner noted that businesses have invested heavily in information technology, but many, particularly those in (other) service industries (e.g., financial services), have not realized expected increases in productivity. In fact, the service sector has experienced a "clear slowdown in productivity," he said, after an "unprecedented spending binge" on information technology. Systems integration can solve this dilemma, but it requires a "back-to-basics questioning" of the functions served by information systems that have often evolved in piecemeal fashion. Needed applications of information technology may be quite different from those considered to be common practice.

Speed is another requisite attribute. Systems-integration firms must meet changing needs and opportunities, placing a "premium on being able to move fast," Turner said. "Solutions to problems that can be solved with yesterday's answers can be provided by the client's own resources."

Given the intricacy of the working relationships between systems-integration firms and their clients and the often substantial investment that integration requires, industry representatives stressed the importance of a local presence in foreign markets. Closeness and longevity of contact can also overcome the suspicion that new entries often encounter in other nations.

DIVERSITY IN THE WORLD MARKET

"Networked computing is a galloping customer requirement" throughout the world, according to Sam R. Willcoxon of AT&T. Ongoing deregulation of telecommunications services in many countries and the confluence of communications and computer technology could fuel "exponential" growth in overseas markets, he said.

In the European Community, the competition facing U.S.-based firms comes from two primary sources. One is in-house competition. Many organizations draw on internal resources and technical staff to design and develop their own systems, according to Heller. "That has always been our [EDS's] competition as we tried to get involved in this business back in the '60s," he said. "So, we feel like from a marketing standpoint, we know how to address in-house competition," he added. Large hardware- and software-manufacturing firms—so-called full-service providers—constitute the other category of competition.

In addition, European firms that produce software are only beginning to expand into systems integration, according to Heller. Several companies have emerged as "formidable" competition in niche markets for specialized systems, such as for computer-aided design and computer-aided manufacturing.

Japan, South Korea, and other Far Eastern nations are more difficult markets for systems-integration firms. Heller described the use of outside firms for internal tasks as "countercultural." "They like doing everything in an integrated sense and for themselves," Heller said. "It is a sign of weakness" to hire an outside firm and entrust a contractor with the responsibility for enhancing functional and strategic capabilities. Nevertheless, EDS has managed to make some inroads in the Japanese market.

Turner added that Price Waterhouse's Japanese office encountered stiff resistance upon its entry into the systems-integration business. Over time, however, the firm's marketing efforts have become progressively more successful.

At this point in the industry's development, as Heller observed, systems integration as an exportable service is largely a U.S. invention that the world market is gradually emulating. AT&T's Willcoxon noted that the concept of systems integration is still evolving, but at a differential pace—faster in the United States than in most other parts of the world. Interestingly, early advances in overseas markets to date have been facilitated by business relationships launched in the United States. For example, the requirement for a local presence overseas by accounting firms like Price Waterhouse that serve multinational clients has provided a springboard for serving foreign clients, a development noted by Turner, while the merger of EDS with General Motors opened doors to new relationships with foreign firms for EDS, according to Heller.

DEPENDENCE ON OTHER COMPUTER-RELATED INDUSTRIES

That the global systems-integration market is poised to take off—offering an "exponential" increase in business opportunities, in Willcoxon's view—is not disputed. Nor is the characterization of U.S.-based enterprises as world leaders in this market. But will the apparent U.S. advantage deteriorate if the underlying industries in the U.S. computer sector—hardware, telecommunications equipment, and software manufacturing—falter in the world marketplace?

Major players in this market acknowledge its dependence on other computer-related industries. Strategically, Heller pointed out, EDS views the health of the other industries in the U.S. computer sector as directly affecting the health of domestic systems-integration firms. "[I]t behooves us to have a very strong force in both software and hardware domestically," Heller said. This is so even though, in the short term, the lower cost or higher quality of some foreign-made goods may influence his firm's buying decisions, or local laws may require use of components manufactured in the home country.

Electronic Data Systems carries "a fair amount of capability in the software arena," Heller noted, "but not to the extent that we want to shift a major portion of our investment into carrying it as fully as the industry itself. In the hardware arena, we have no interest in that kind of shift in capital investment. So, long term, we are willing, able, capable, and have the intention of supporting the domestic capability, whether that means in terms of our dollars, our energy, or our political influence. . . . [W]e see it as a team effort."

STANDARDIZATION

On scales small and large, systems integration is made easier by standards: The greater the level of standardization, the greater the level of interoperability between computers and other digital devices as well. Today, as noted in earlier chapters, idiosyncracy rather than standardization is the norm, and systems-integration firms have devoted some of their resources to overcoming barriers to compatibility. "We have had to formulate solutions where standards didn't exist," Heller said. From an industrywide perspective, the process may be inefficient, a duplication of investment and effort. Standards can motivate innovation by serving, explained Heller, "as the act of declaring innovation significant . . . , [establishing] a benchmark that the next round of innovation must significantly surpass—or leapfrog—or sidestep." But without adequate safeguards for protecting intellectual property, according to Heller, standardization will quicken the transfer of innovations from inventor to imitator. Therefore, if standardization is to increase, there must be stronger safeguards for preserving the returns to innovation and greater international compliance with those laws, in Heller's view.

AT&T's Willcoxon contended that without greater standardization, the "magnificent opportunity for productivity improvement" that computers afford would go largely unrealized. "Users are beginning to reject closed proprietary systems that isolate their data in computers that can't talk to each other," he said, adding that clients want to "mix, match, and interconnect products from whatever vendors meet their needs."

Standards are critical to meeting customers' varied needs, enabling the information industry to "really begin to deliver on its promises," according to Willcoxon. Willcoxon called for an "enlightened combination of cooperation and competition." He said that firms must cooperate in developing and selecting appropriate standards and then compete in "devising solutions that are best tailored to user needs."

Turner of Price Waterhouse offered a complementary view. While acknowledging fears that standards may hurt innovative software and hardware companies, he urged firms to view the issue from the perspective of users who have invested heavily in information technology but who have not reaped the anticipated benefits. If standards can deliver "better productivity enhancement," then firms must accede or risk "increasing dissatisfaction from users."

But would high levels of compatibility between the computer and telecommunications equipment of different vendors eliminate the need for systems-integration firms? Absolutely not, according to industry representatives. "[T]here are a lot more things involved than just whether boxes and software hook together compatibly," Heller said. The "real value-added" part of systems integration is the "understanding of the problem you are trying to solve."

Given the number of hardware and software options facing customers and the many potential approaches to solving a problem, systems-integration firms are not likely to see complexity or demand for their services evaporate with increasing standardization, according to Heller and other industry representatives. Raj Reddy of Carnegie Mellon University shared the following analogy: "Just because you have a vocabulary and a language and a syntax and a dictionary, it doesn't mean you can write a best-selling novel. A best-selling novel is the composition of these things in ways that make an attractive plot and a solution and various other things. I think no matter how many standards you have, you still have that problem of creating the best-selling plot and novel. That is the systems-integration business."

Perhaps, as several colloquium participants suggested, the debate over standards should shift from whether they are needed to how standards are developed and how they influence innovation and technological progress. Robert E. Kahn, president of the Corporation for National Research Initiatives, suggested that rather than viewing them as "unchanging over time," standards should be considered dynamic, evolving in step with technology. With a flexible standard-setting system, the "critical issue" becomes how to manage standards so they accommodate change, in Kahn's view.

INFRASTRUCTURE FOR THE INFORMATION AGE

Firms that specialize in computer and communications services are, in effect, building an Information Age equivalent of the highway system, an infrastructure that accommodates the flow of information in textual, graphic, and voice form. Systems-integration firms, for example, link once-independent islands of hardware, applications, and their specialized domains of software into a functioning whole, just as roads connect previously isolated communities into zones of commerce. Like the businesses that now line many stretches of the nation's highway system, a growing array of electronic databases and other specialized services have sprouted up to serve an increasing number of users whose computers are connected to networks.

Colloquium participants argued that this movement toward network-based enhancement and integration of computer and communication capabilities is proceeding much more haphazardly than did the development of the national highway system; the full promise of networked computing—in which one computer can communicate with any other, regardless of its location or its type—is far from being fulfilled. Many obstacles stand in the way of making computer-to-computer communication as easy as making a telephone call. The potential economic advantages of a nationwide information network appear to be motivating Japan and Western European countries to begin developing the necessary infrastructure. In the United States, where the geographic scope and scale of the task and its cost are significantly greater, a cohesive approach is lacking.

In recent years several groups, including the Computer Science and Technology Board, have called for the development of a national information infrastructure or a partial implementation of this concept devoted to the support of research and development.[5,6] At the colloquium, Charles Ferguson of MIT explicitly advocated a government-coordinated program to build a nationwide advanced-technology computer communications infrastructure over the next one or two decades. The network would be the conduit for communications required by an ever-growing number and variety of digital devices, from computers and telephones to high-definition television sets.

According to Ferguson, a national information infrastructure will not only become an economic necessity, but its development also will be a direct stimulus to a "very wide spectrum of information- and technology-intensive industries." Manufacturers of base technologies—for semiconductor packaging, automated assembly, optoelectronics, and production of printed circuit boards and fiberoptic cable—would benefit from infrastructure-oriented research projects and, ultimately, from the demand generated by the actual construction and implementation of the network and the associated user equipment. Moreover, the proposed network could be the means for U.S. reentry into markets for consumer electronic equipment, which increasingly incorporates the same digital technologies used in computers (see Chapter 2).

Some colloquium participants equated a government-led project to build a national information infrastructure with the U.S. decision in the early 1960s to send astronauts to the moon by the end of the decade. The "symbolic value" alone of such a project could "galvanize the technical community" and the rest of the country, suggested Wladawsky-Berger of IBM. But more important, Wladawsky-Berger and others stressed, is the great underlying utility of having a networked economy. "If U.S. industry generally is served by inferior networks and digital systems," Ferguson has written, "the economy will suffer. Conversely, if the United States were to possess the world's most advanced [information] infrastructure, the economy would benefit, and so probably would U.S. vendors of digital information systems."[7]

One significant benefit would be to open up new markets for information and information-processing products—markets that the United States might understand and exploit before foreign competition does. A possibility is to computerize commerce, using digital communications among computers acting as agents

for companies to find suppliers, determine price and availability of parts, nego-
tiate deliveries, convey shipping information, and deal with problems. This
array of services goes far beyond what electronic data interchange achieves
today. It is an example of the kind of service that needs careful fostering by
government and other institutions; it is not simply a university research project.

Although no one at the colloquium opposed the idea of a national information infrastructure, levels of enthusiasm for the concept varied. Heller of EDS
advised proponents to define clearly the national purpose that would be served
by such a network. He also cautioned that private firms would not embrace the
proposal without government leadership and government-sponsored incentives
for companies that contribute to developing a public good. Without incentives,
firms will act in their own self-interest and avoid projects that do not benefit
them directly.

Proponents of a national information network also injected cautionary notes
into their endorsements of the concept. For example, Stardent Computer's
Gordon Bell, who helped craft a proposal for a national research and education
network while he was an assistant director of the National Science Foundation,
warned that continuing erosion of the nation's manufacturing base may mean
that many infrastructural components, such as switches and optical fiber, may
have to be purchased from foreign suppliers. He also advised focusing first on
networking for researchers, to avoid making the task so large and complex as to
be unmanageable.

Ferguson of MIT has cautioned that if proprietary controls of network-orient-
ed cooperative research projects are lax, foreign firms may benefit more than
U.S. participants. There is also the danger, he maintained, that policies intended
to preserve the U.S. market for domestic firms could result in "crude protection-
ism." If policies are designed to benefit only a few selected industries, the competitiveness of others that produce goods and services based on digital technologies could suffer, Ferguson suggested. A potential outcome is greater foreign
penetration of U.S. computer and networking markets, in his view.

"I think it is the government's business to provide infrastructure," said
Robert W. Lucky, executive director of the communication sciences research
division at AT&T Bell Laboratories. "I don't think there is money in this right
now, but I think the nation needs it. . . . [W]hat it requires, I think, is government leadership, not government regulation."

NOTES

1.   U.S. Department of Commerce. "Information Services," *1989 U.S. Industrial
     Outlook,* (Washington, D.C., 1989), p. 45-2.
2.   U.S. Department of Commerce, *1989 U.S. Industrial Outlook,* p. 45-4.
3.   U.S. Department of Commerce, *1989 U.S. Industrial Outlook,* p. 45-4.
4.   U.S. Department of Commerce, *1989 U.S. Industrial Outlook,* p. 45-2.

5. Computer Science and Technology Board, National Research Council. *The National Challenge in Computer Science and Technology* (Washington, D.C.: National Academy Press, 1988).
6. Computer Science and Technology Board, National Research Council. *Toward a National Research Network* (Washington, D.C.: National Academy Press, 1988).
7. Ferguson, Charles H. "HDTV, Digital Communications, and Competitiveness: Implications for U.S. High Technology Policy," VLSI Memo No. 89-506, Massachusetts Institute of Technology, VLSI Publications, February, 1989, p. 6.

5
Business and Marketing

The market is the final judge of a firm's caliber—its ability to manage its capital and human resources to develop and produce goods and services tailored to the preferences of consumers—and the competitiveness of an industry reflects the capabilities of its constituent firms. In growing industries, innovation can be a prime determinant of marketing success. As an industry matures, however, manufacturing efficiency, sales, marketing, and other factors become the critical ingredients of competitiveness. "In many cases," observed Lawrence Tesler of Apple Computer, "we lost our competitive edge not because of technology, but because of better management and smarter strategy."

"Increasingly, market success depends on early product introduction to determine customer requirements," observed William J. Spencer of Xerox. "The lessons learned from selling and servicing your own product and watching competitors must be quickly incorporated into product changes that meet market needs. The high content of electronics and software in current and future systems will lead to ever more rapid introduction of new products and an increased requirement to respond in shorter times to market needs."

Spencer added that, unfortunately, many of the now-essential attributes for competing in domestic and global markets—"listening to customers, learning from the market, and quick reactions"—are "not the hallmarks of U.S. corporations." The consequences of this deficiency can be "loss of market share, lower revenues and profits, and an inability to support long-term initiatives, including R&D in U.S. corporations."

Colloquium participants focused on the causes and symptoms of flagging competitiveness in important computer sector industries. Like Spencer, many saw overarching problems, difficulties spanning many parts of the U.S. economy but perhaps imposing an especially heavy toll on the research-intensive computer sector. For example, John L. Doyle of Hewlett Packard advised his business counterparts, as well as government officials, to heed the findings of the President's Commission on Industrial Competitiveness.[1] That body found, Doyle said, "four causes of U.S. industrial decline: failure to develop human resources as well as our competition, inadequate incentives for saving and investment, trade policies that failed to recognize global reality, and a slowness in the commercialization of new technology." Of overriding concern to individual firms, he suggested, is the failure of many to integrate manufacturing with development.

"It has been said that the manufacturing industry has passed through three phases, pursuing efficiency, quality, flexibility, and now innovation," Doyle said. "But these are not alternatives. They are cumulative, and competitiveness demands improvements in all four."

Discussions at the colloquium focused on several key problems that, if uncorrected, will continue to hamper the performance of individual firms and the computer sector as a whole.

ISOLATING THE ISSUES

Technology Management and Transfer

Success, says an adage, has many owners. This timeless insight has taken an ironic twist in the computer sector. U.S. enterprises, sometimes building on research performed at the nation's universities, have spawned many commercially successful innovations. Innovative firms may receive proper acknowledgment for their path-breaking efforts, but, too often, foreign companies have claimed the commercial rewards of invention.

A growing body of business literature has documented the failure of U.S. firms to capitalize on innovations that later proved tremendously successful in foreign-manufactured consumer products. Among the many legendary examples is the Japanese dominance of global markets for video recorders, invented by the Ampex Corporation in 1956. Through the 1960s, the California firm claimed a 70 percent share of the world market for video recording technology. Then came the video cassette recorder (VCR), an industrywide, standardized format that suddenly eclipsed Ampex's proprietary format and attracted many competitors.

"[T]he basis of competition quickly became manufacturing and the ability to move quickly through the design cycle," recounted Richard S. Rosenbloom, professor at Harvard's Graduate School of Business Administration. "What had been a six-year product life cycle collapsed to six months. Ampex never developed the skills needed to compete in that kind of business, never anticipated that its business could come that way, and found itself very quickly limited to a narrow and shrinking niche in an industry that it created and which expanded a hundredfold as a result of its technology."

Obviously, VCRs are not computers, although the technological similarities between the two are increasing. Nevertheless, the problems that confounded Ampex are not unique to VCRs, or even to the broader consumer electronics industry, Rosenbloom maintained. "I think that is a story," he said, "that can happen throughout the information products industries to companies that are banking on sustaining proprietary positions and banking on a set of skills that have served them well to date but that are not guaranteed to serve them in the future."

Addressing the same issue from a different angle, Rosenbloom noted that some of the largest businesses in the computer sector have failed in major efforts to diversify into new markets. IBM's venture into telecommunications, AT&T's move into the merchant market for memory chips, and Xerox's attempt to branch into workstation production failed to fulfill expectations for reasons other than a lack of technological expertise, Rosenbloom suggested. "They had no trouble grasping intellectually the science and technology of those new businesses," he explained, "but somewhere they lacked the industrial capacity to establish a competitive advantage in a marketplace that called for something different from what they were offering."

"There is more than random error here," he said. The direct causes of the "persistent failure of leading firms to adopt new technology that has later proven astonishingly important to the industry" remain elusive, according to Rosenbloom. He speculated that part of the problem may be endemic to the American style of management and perhaps to the way managers are educated and trained. But remedies will not be forthcoming until the problem is thoroughly understood, he maintained. "There is something systematically vulnerable about the way American companies have built positions in industrial markets and have tried to sustain their dominance in those markets," Rosenbloom said.

Clues may come from tracing the often-fragmented lineage of commercially valuable technologies. James H. Morris of Carnegie Mellon University described the evolution of the user-friendly human interface embodied in Apple's highly successful family of Macintosh computers. Like many other innovations, it originated in an organization that can lay claim to many of the technological advances that underlie successful products, but the innovating firm did not guide the technology to commercial fruition.

Morris traced the roots of the successful user interface, which is characterized by a bit-map display, a pointing device ("mouse") for guiding the cursor, and screen "windows," to federally funded research conducted at the Stanford Research Institute (now SRI International) during the late 1960s. A collaborative project between SRI and the Xerox Palo Alto Research Center essentially transferred the technology to Xerox Corp., which continued the effort and drew on programming developments in Europe and at U.S. universities. Many of the embryonic components of the user interface technology were embodied in Xerox's experimental ALTO computer of the early 1970s. Eventually, the company introduced the Xerox 8010 Star System, the first commercial product to feature the interface that is now used in virtually all computer workstations (see Figure 5.1).

The Star System represented a major advance in commercial technology, according to Morris, who was involved in the product's development, but it was too expensive. "We didn't think about marketing and the cost of these things," said Morris. He attributed this "marketing myopia" to most of the staff's previous experience in research funded by the Department of Defense, where cost considerations often do not enter into evaluations of a system's performance.

Through circuitous events, the approach pioneered at Xerox was eventually perfected at Apple, but success was not immediate. The Lisa computer, Apple's

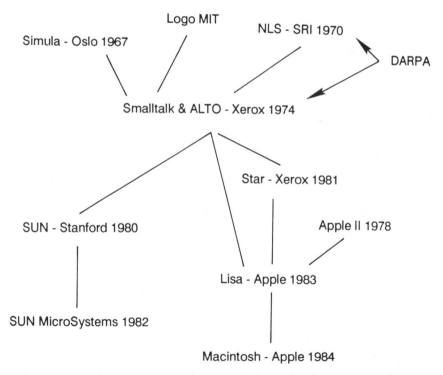

FIGURE 5.1 Key technology transfer paths leading to the Macintosh series of computers. SOURCE: Courtesy of James Morris, Carnegie Mellon University, 1989.

first product with the advanced human interface, did not win many customers, but a subsequent introduction, the Macintosh, has helped the company secure a significant share of the global market for personal computers.

Morris's examination of failed attempts to transfer technology internally yielded several common themes. Contrary to conventional thinking, Morris explained, many commercially successful ideas—at least in the software industry—did not originate with small start-up firms, but rather they were the offspring of "rather large research investments made by rather big companies." Start-up firms, however, often succeeded where established firms failed: They developed good ideas into cost-effective products.

Morris speculated that large firms may fail to capitalize on promising innovations because their attention is divided among many product lines. As a result, they may overlook a line of research that is ripe for development; in contrast, a small firm that seizes a good idea concentrates almost entirely on developing the innovation. Perhaps that is why technology transfers between firms—what Morris called "hostile transfers"—are more successful than those that are attempted internally.

Moreover, a firm that capitalizes on an innovation pioneered elsewhere is not limited to using an idea in its original form. "If somebody is taking something without permission," Morris said, "they are free to pick and choose what they take and don't take." The same may apply to foreign firms that capitalize on research developments pioneered in the United States. Their selections and adoptions of U.S. technologies are likely to be guided by marketing considerations that innovating firms fail to recognize, according to Morris.

To the benefit of the U.S. computer sector, greater emphasis on cooperative research could promote technology transfer in the United States, Morris suggested; "intermixing" of organizations and technologists appears to facilitate the kind of "creative technology transfer" that U.S. firms have found so difficult to do internally. In addition, with Japan and other nations challenging or overtaking U.S. leadership in key areas of technology, U.S. firms should broaden their purview of science and engineering research, Morris advised. U.S. firms should be just as quick to exploit commercially promising innovations that originate overseas as foreign firms are to capitalize on the results of research done in the United States. "In some sense," Morris observed, "grabbing something from another country . . . is a more powerful and better thing to do." John Doyle of Hewlett Packard was even more direct: "I believe that not legally using good ideas from our competitive products is improvident."

Harnessing Complementary Assets

Even if firms master the complexities of innovation and technology transfer, there is no guarantee that they will succeed in the market. "[M]any of the ideas and products—once introduced to the market and, often, before they are introduced—are essentially available to everyone," explained David J. Teece of the University of California at Berkeley. "They can be reverse engineered, they can be improved upon, and so forth."

Unless an innovative firm controls or has access to all the necessary "complementary assets," Teece said, such as specialized manufacturing capabilities and well-developed distribution and marketing channels, it will not realize the commercial benefits of its R&D accomplishments. Instead, those benefits will flow to "imitator" or "follow-up" firms that have harnessed these complementary capabilities, Teece explained.

Much of the success of Japanese firms in global markets can be attributed to their mastery of the competitive elements that support the commercialization of innovations. Design cycles and the time needed to develop manufacturing proficiency for a new product are often faster in Japan than in the United States. "Therefore, [Japanese firms] can take what is best out there in the world stock of knowledge and bring it into the market ahead of the competition and take a good chunk of the market," Teece said.

Given the success of this approach, it is not surprising that Japanese firms invest the bulk of their R&D dollars in process improvements. The attention to process extends even to the processes of research and development. The penetration of supercomputing, for example, into electronics and automotive R&D in Japan suggests a Japanese advantage in applying advanced tools to improve design innovation, reduce production time, and improve quality. In the United States, firms tend to allocate most of their R&D dollars to developing new products. If U.S. firms do not devote more resources to developing manufacturing competence and other complementary capabilities, continued investment in product-oriented research could be self-defeating because results will quickly be transferred to competitors, Teece maintained. If a firm innovates, it must "simultaneously be in a position" to commercialize the innovation, he observed.

The integrated structure of Japanese firms and industries facilitates rapid product introduction because it facilitates the harnessing of complementary assets. For example, many of Japan's electronics firms manufacture semiconductors and other components as well as the computers and other products that use such devices. In addition, these firms often have partial-equity shares in companies that produce needed specialized assets, such as semiconductor-manufacturing equipment. Moreover, competing firms develop relationships to address issues of mutual concern.

Most firms in the U.S. computer sector control few of the specialized complementary capabilities that Teece believes are necessary for competing in global markets. This may reflect, in part, a lack of vertical integration. In the United States, IBM may be the only computer sector firm that has achieved levels of integration comparable to those of the larger Japanese electronic firms. It is hardly self-sufficient, however. Recognition of that fact may explain why IBM has assumed a leading role in forging cooperative relationships among U.S. hardware manufacturers.

Teece argued further that the computer sector as a whole is losing complementary capabilities. As the sector's domestic infrastructure of materials, component, and equipment suppliers erodes, its ability to compete will also deteriorate, even if U.S. firms continue to be prodigious sources of innovations.

This point was also noted by Yale's Perlis, who observed that "the thing that we seem to be losing to the Japanese is the infrastructure that is most important. It is nice that IBM can make everything from 'A to Z' and that other companies exist. What is most important is that, when they look around for some activity, technique, [or] equipment that they need to fulfill an idea to produce something worthwhile, it will not be there. They will have to spend large amounts of time, funds, and energy to gather what should have been around the corner."

In his writings, Teece has disputed the "notion that the United States can adopt a 'designer role' in international commerce while letting independent firms in countries such as Japan, [South] Korea, Taiwan, or Mexico do the manufacturing."[2] In the long run, he believes, the majority of benefits will flow to the firms that make the products rather than to the companies that supply designs or other knowledge-based, intangible assets "whose true performance features are difficult to predict."

A somewhat different view was offered by Joel Birnbaum, vice president and general manager of Hewlett Packard's information architecture group. If a firm buys components from foreign suppliers, he contended, it still can succeed in designing and marketing systems. Birnbaum used Hewlett Packard's popular Laser Jet printer as an example, which was also cited earlier in the colloquium by another speaker, of how U.S. firms are becoming increasingly reliant on foreign manufacturers of components. "We buy the print mechanism from Canon, but we did a much better job than they did of figuring out what goes around it, the page definition formats, how to service it, how to document it, how to package it, how to market it, and how to manufacture the entire product." The result is a high value-added product, one with annual sales exceeding $1 billion. According to Birnbaum, standardization accommodates the development of value-added products and services, allowing firms to use the best components the international market has to offer and to sell their products throughout the world.

Complementary capabilities will become especially critical as more computer products evolve into commodity products, as many at the colloquium predicted. In commodity markets, Teece said, "manufacturing matters. That is where marketing matters. That is where many other things [besides innovation] matter. So, while one cannot in general say that manufacturing always matters, I think it matters in this industry, . . . where one doesn't have good intellectual property protection." Strengthening international intellectual property laws would benefit innovative firms, he added, but there are "inherent limits" to safeguards that might be extended to intellectual property.

An Argument for Cooperation

The importance of complementary assets suggests that a promising avenue to maintaining a competitive U.S. computer sector is cooperation. Cooperation between manufacturers and suppliers and even between competitors can effect a sharing of some complementary assets. Recognizing this possibility, many U.S. enterprises have turned to foreign firms, allowing their technologies to be licensed in exchange for manufacturing expertise and capital. But failure to cooperate and to make necessary assets available domestically results in tactical decisions that benefit individual firms but may eventually harm the entire sector.

Thus, as the international push for standardization grows and as computers come to resemble consumer commodities, "cooperation becomes increasingly important," facilitating the strategic thinking and investments that were absent during Japan's rise to dominance in DRAM production, Teece maintained. Changes in management styles and in policies governing the structure of U.S. industry will be needed to achieve the levels of cooperation that global competition demands, he added. For example, perceptions about the constraints resulting from antitrust laws may discourage cooperation, although the laws actually allow a wide range of mergers, joint ventures, and so on.

Teece also stressed the importance of integrating science policy and technology policy, which now overlap only slightly. "If you don't connect the development of scientific capability with technological capability, there won't be too many national benefits," he said. According to computer sector representatives, that link must extend to the federal research laboratories. Several criticized the paucity of commercially relevant technologies that have been generated by the laboratories. To date, argued Hewlett Packard's Doyle, the returns from research conducted at the more than 700 tax-payer-supported facilities have not been commensurate with the nation's annual investment of about $20 billion.

Managerial Incentives and Short Time Horizons

United States business as a whole is consistently criticized as being myopic, focusing on short-term gains at the expense of long-term competitiveness. The computer sector is no exception, according to colloquium participants. Nor has it escaped the consequences of this short-term outlook that are most evident, perhaps, in the deterioration of the manufacturing base.

But is there a single, fundamental cause of the problem? The list of detrimental influences includes the federal budget deficit, tax policies that encourage consumer spending over saving, stockholders' expectations for immediate returns on their investments, managers' emphasis on high quarterly and annual profits and neglect of investments in equipment and R&D projects that are critical not to next year's profit statement but to their firms' performance three or more years down the road. Perhaps, as several studies have suggested, this tendency to risk the future for short-term gain reflects, in part, attitudes imparted during managers' educational training.

All of these factors, and probably others, contribute to the short time horizons of U.S. firms. Sorting through the list and assigning the proportion of blame attributable to each factor diverts attention from the critical task of addressing the problem in all areas. As colloquium participants noted, the issue is clearly recognized as one directly affecting the health of the entire computer industry. Each responsible party, from the federal government to individual firms, must act, participants emphasized. Otherwise, U.S. firms will continue "to optimize locally," not globally, and foreign companies that act on the basis of long-term, strategic interests will continue to gain in markets.

At the level of the individual firm, both Ferguson and Teece recommended evaluating the incentives that guide management decisions. For example, the short-term emphasis of U.S. managers, Teece suggested, "may be due to the fact that their incentive structure is weighted, in some cases at least, too heavily in favor of salary and not enough in terms of stock."

Learning from Failure and Responding to the Market

Interpreting the results of his own studies and that of other researchers, MIT's Ferguson described the emergence of an approach to manufacturing management that is now well established in Japan, is currently being adopted in South Korea and Taiwan, but is uncommon in the United States. The hallmarks of the approach are short design cycles due to the partial sharing of different product designs, close coordination between design and manufacturing, and a very flexible manufacturing system.

One attribute of the Japanese system is that it accommodates failure, several speakers noted. "In the VCR story," said Harvard's Rosenbloom, "there were three generations of VCRs that the Japanese, particularly Sony, introduced before they finally got to the one that worked, and each time they learned some things that were very important in developing the next generation." "Failure," he added, "is an inherent part of learning, which is an inherent part of innovation."

Doyle pointed out, however, that the consequences of introducing a poorly received product differ among markets. In contrast to commodity consumer electronic goods, high-cost products for business customers leave little margin for error. For now, design and development cycles for business computer systems, Doyle suggested, must be longer than those for consumer products. However, he added, "the trouble is that industrial marketing [appears] to be moving closer to consumer marketing." Rapid product development could become more important, placing U.S. firms at a disadvantage.

The Role of Small Entrepreneurial Firms

Small entrepreneurial firms have been popularly associated with the vitality of the U.S. computer sector. To their credit, they have been the wellspring of many of the innovations that have paced the technological and market advances of computer-related products. However, recent competitive shifts have brought to light the limitations of smaller firms and the consequences of assuming that their strengths will preserve the interests of domestic industries overall.

In retrospect, for example, start-up semiconductor firms appear to have destabilized the industry and have lacked the resources to continue developing the manufacturing expertise necessary to stave off the challenges of better-financed and better-organized Japanese competitors.[3] Had the U.S. semiconductor industry undergone consolidation, the argument continues, the resultant vertically integrated firms would have been in a strategic position to meet the competitive challenge.

The history of the semiconductor industry also supports a contrary view: Large U.S. firms may not be dynamic enough to compete in the rapidly changing industry. Many conglomerates and large U.S. electronics firms did diversify into semiconductor manufacturing, but most eventually withdrew. IBM is the most notable exception. Looking at the computer sector more broadly, there is the problem, previously noted, of an inability of large firms to capitalize quickly on innovation. As Carnegie Mellon's Morris observed, while many innovations originated in large firms, their successful commercialization was often realized by small start-up companies (see above, "Technology Management and Transfer" section of this chapter).

These events present a quandary. "In the United States," Ferguson said, "there is the striking fact that a very disproportionate fraction of innovation and newness comes from small entrepreneurial firms." The phenomenon appears unique to the United States. "That is not the case in Japan or [South] Korea," Ferguson added. "Korean manufacturing is dominated by four vertically integrated, diversified industrial complexes. In Japan, eight firms account for most electronics production. The smallest of them [has annual revenues] of $10 billion."

Gordon Bell of Stardent Computer stressed the importance of small firms in computer manufacturing, arguing that productivity is "inversely proportional to size. . . . I have been in two start-ups, each with 50 engineers," he said, "and I assure you I could not have done those same projects in a large organization with 500 people. It would have taken twice as long, and the quality would not be the same."

Colloquium participants did not dispute the firm-size dichotomy and its apparent relationship to innovation. The general failure of large U.S. firms to demonstrate the same speed in reacting to the market as their Asian counterparts, several suggested, stems from management and organizational problems. Compared with companies that have flat management structures and only a few integrated divisions, hierarchically structured firms lack the cohesion and versatility needed to respond quickly to market opportunities.

"I would argue," said William R. Hambrecht, president and co-chief executive officer of the venture capital firm Hambrecht & Quist, "that the entrepreneurial young company has done a good job of competing . . . because [it] is usually the ultimate integrated business unit. It has representations from other functions, but they are all in one room."

Also troubling to computer sector representatives was the apparently increasing prevalence of foreign investment in small high-technology companies. In exchange for needed capital and, perhaps, manufacturing expertise, these start-up firms are often licensing their technology to foreign firms, which may later emerge as competitors. (It should be noted, however, that licensing arrangements may be the only option for entering a foreign market in which access is government controlled.)

Foreign firms find the United States to be a very attractive place to shop for new ideas, Ferguson added. To underscore his point, Ferguson told of a Japanese firm that was setting up a holding company in the United States to invest in new technology in computer and other areas. The firm allocated $2 billion for this purpose, he noted.

Unfortunately, established U.S. firms have been less receptive than their foreign competitors to small firms seeking assistance to develop their ideas. One factor that may contribute to this reluctance is that pioneering new technologies entails risks. An established firm may forego the chance to make a technological leap, deciding instead to respond if and when an innovation proves commercially promising. Another factor may be the so-called "Arrow effect," which suggests that market-leading firms benefit by slowing the rate of technological advance.[4]

Hambrecht suggested that established U.S. firms have begun to change their views on entrepreneurial firms. In recent years, he said, large firms have demonstrated "growing acceptance . . . that entrepreneurial companies are good places to develop products" and look at them "less as threats and more as partners."

CONSOLIDATION AHEAD?

Venture capital provided much of the seed money that led to the U.S. computer sector's flush of growth during the 1970s and early 1980s, giving rise to such firms as Digital Equipment Corporation, Apple Computer, Microsoft, and Sun Microsystems. According to Hambrecht, the flurry of new company formation is ebbing, and today's start-up firms will often face formidable obstacles.

Much of the nation's estimated $40 billion pool of private venture capital has been invested in the computer sector, to the point of overstimulating entry of new companies, Hambrecht maintained (see Figure 5.2). Returns to investors have fallen dramatically since the late 1970s, and the numerous new companies created with the influx of venture capital have made it increasingly difficult for today's start-up firms to carve out a market niche that offers the potential for above-average earnings growth.

"[E]ven when we were right," Hambrecht explained, "even when we picked the right people in the right niche at the right time, and they [the start-up firms] executed well . . . they found a crowded landscape. . . instead of having a reasonably free run to exploit their product position, they were in a corporate dogfight."

With fewer apparent opportunities available to potential start-up firms, investors have soured on the computer sector and, according to Hambrecht, the sector may not regain its allure. One reason for this outlook is the shortened horizons of venture capital funds. In principle, venture capital is invested with the aim of long-term earnings growth. But increasingly, investors expect quick returns, and they have become more averse to risk. Fund managers are responding in kind, Hambrecht added.

In Hambrecht's view, the hardware-manufacturing industry has begun to mature, and forces of consolidation are already in evidence. Computer manufacturing continues to outperform other parts of the economy, but annual rates of revenue growth in many segments of the industry are about half of what they were in the late 1970s. Moreover, costs of entry have soared, not only for equipment but also for setting up marketing channels and other components. Hambrecht noted that Intel began manufacturing semiconductors in 1968 with an initial investment of $3 million. Today, building and equipping a modern semiconductor plant would cost about $300 million.

Another deterrent to starting new companies in the hardware industry is standardization. Acknowledging the arguments for and against standardization, Hambrecht said his firm has decided that "standards are a way of life and standards mean hardware becomes a commodity." Opportunities to develop computers that surpass standardized versions and gain market acceptance will be few, he predicted.

Given these trends, formation of new companies will continue to slow, and intraindustry mergers—"the strong buying the weak"—will increase, according to Hambrecht. In the short-term, consolidation will appear to promote greater efficiency in the industry, he explained, noting that a reduced flow of venture capital creates the need for more cooperation within an industry. Hambrecht also sounded a warning, however: As the entry of new firms decreases, established firms will slow their product development efforts to increase their

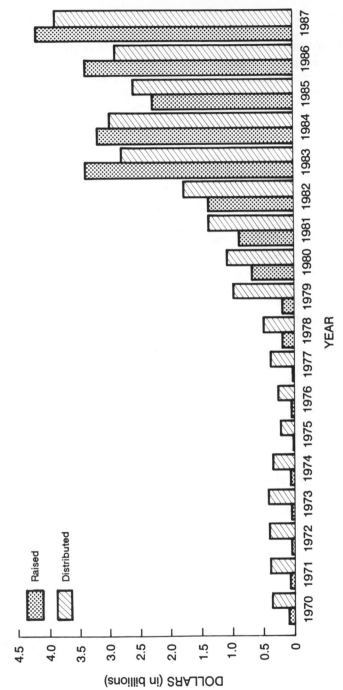

FIGURE 5.2 Venture capital raised and distributed in the United States. SOURCE: Courtesy of Hambrecht & Quist, 1989.

returns. This situation, akin to the experiences of the U.S. automobile, textile, and consumer electronics industries, sets the stage for increased competition from foreign firms, according to Hambrecht.

Hambrecht's outlook for the software industry is considerably brighter. Software innovation, he believes, is the key to "above-average profitability and the ability to build a truly successful business"—although they do not now, investors will eventually recognize the growth potential of software development.

NOTES

1. President's Commission on Industrial Competitiveness. *Global Competition: The New Reality* (Washington, D.C.: Government Printing Office, 1985).
2. David J. Teece. "Capturing Value from Technological Innovation: Integration, Strategic Partnering, and Licensing Decisions," in *Technology and Global Industry,* Bruce R. Guile and Harvey Brooks, eds. (Washington, D.C.: National Academy Press, 1987), pp. 91-92.
3. Dertouzos, Michael L., Richard K. Lester, Robert M. Solow, MIT Commission on Industrial Productivity. *Made in America: Regaining the Productive Edge* (Cambridge, Mass.: MIT Press, 1989), p. 256.
4. As Kenneth Flamm explains the Arrow effect, "For the established leader, a new product may very well compete with its existing product lines in some markets. Profits on the new product are then partially offset by lost profits on other offerings. For a new entrant, there is no offsetting loss, and the perceived return to entry will be higher" (Kenneth Flamm, *Creating the Computer,* Washington, D.C.: Brookings Institution, 1988, p. 227).

6

Turning Point

The maturation of the computer sector and the escalation of foreign competition place the sector at a turning point. U.S. semiconductor manufacturers and their suppliers face the prospect of continuing losses of market share to foreign firms. In turn, manufacturers of computers and related equipment find their base of domestic support eroding as competitors strengthen theirs. For now, the nation's software, services, and systems-integration industries sit atop global markets, but given events in other parts of the sector and developments abroad, one feels compelled to ask, For how long?

Building on strengths, overcoming existing problems, and averting new ones require "a massive change in thinking," noted AT&T's Lucky. "I am left with the sense that we have a consensus on what is wrong," he said, reflecting on conditions in the hardware industry, "but no collective will to do anything about it."

The history of numerous other industries and the observations of all colloquium participants underscore how difficult significant change will be to achieve. As Harvard's Rosenbloom described it, "[T]here is something systematically vulnerable about the way American companies have built positions in industrial markets and have tried to sustain dominance in those markets."

The computer sector is saddled with perceptions from its earlier years that may no longer be appropriate and that may motivate a complacency among policymakers that is unwarranted, in view of current realities. For example, "We have become slaves to the image of the entrepreneur shaping technology—the garage computer or spreadsheet software package," warned Belady of MCC. "Unfortunately, many software projects, especially those having considerable risk and which have lengthy development periods, cannot emerge from such an environment. Bits and pieces from the academic side have difficulty getting integrated. The massive efforts aiming at improved tools and techniques for complex system design and sustained by long-term stable funding at [Japanese] companies . . . have few counterparts in the United States."

The U.S. computer sector is too large and too complex to link the fortunes of each its three major industry groups—hardware, software, and services and systems integration—in a dominolike fashion. Yet as representatives from each industry group pointed out at the colloquium, there are strategic dependencies common to all. And these dependencies are likely to grow as technology, the terms of competition, and the structure of the sector change at a rapid rate, one of the hallmarks of the sector. Therefore troubles in one industry can have implications for all and, as computing becomes more pervasive, for the entire economy.

AN ASSET AT RISK

The woes of the U.S. semiconductor and semiconductor-manufacturing-equipment industries focus concern on another major chunk of the hardware industry, computer manufacturers. If U.S. computer manufacturers were to surrender their leading position in global markets, would the consequences be any worse than those wrought by market declines in steel or other mature industries? If computer manufacturing is indeed becoming a mature industry, as Hambrecht and others maintained, might it not be more efficient to use computers that are manufactured elsewhere, freeing up resources for production of higher-value-added goods and services? These questions are not uncommon.

"There are a lot of people who are still not convinced that there is a problem—that manufacturing needs to be preserved—and those people are in influential positions, making decisions in the government," said John E. McPhee, director of the Office of Computers and Business Equipment at the Department of Commerce.

Colloquium participants shared the view that a narrow economic analysis focusing on comparative production efficiencies across countries ignores the rationale for a more strategic perspective. Computer development and manufacturing are not simply ends in themselves—although they are nontrivial ends in terms of their contribution to the GNP, the balance of trade, employment, and other conventional measures. Rather, they are intricately linked both to the development of other computer-related products, including software and services as well as other types of hardware, and to advances in the use of computer technology. The use of computers contributes increasingly to the competitiveness of virtually all industries. In short, computers themselves are an engine of technological change, a prerequisite for national growth in a global economy.

The special and increasingly intrinsic value of computer-related technologies was captured by Perlis of Yale.

The computer is a tool of thought and function. It helps us model and it itself is modeled. As an agent of control it permits us to interact with nature at all levels of granularity from the stars to the quarks. The computer is crucial in our effort to escape from the biological polyhedron that evolution has consigned us to: It is crucial in the operations that extend the temperature range, the atmospheric pressures, the years of life, the atmosphere, and the health that are required for us to continue to exist. We must never forget that we are at the beginning of the Computer Age, so that exploration of its role must continue into the foreseeable future. Thus the physical form of the computer may change, but our recognition of and dependence on the abstract concept "computation" will continue to deepen. It is inconceivable that we could function without the computer. Of course we must not worship the machine as an idol but we must domesticate it so that it serves both as a good and as a performer. The computer must be expected to play a role in almost every human activity.

It is because of the growing pervasiveness of computing, argued Perlis and others, that we cannot yield a leadership role complacently. "For the computer industry," commented Perlis, "yielding control to foreign concerns will have an impact in the intellectual sense that yielding agriculture would have in the biological sense." Echoed Teece from the University of California at Berkeley, "The computer industry generates significant positive technological and market demand spillovers to other industries. Moreover, for a nation to capture these spillovers, it is necessary to have a domestic computer industry."

Despite the great progress that has been made in making computers easier to use and finding new ways to use them, colloquium participants acknowledged that businesses and individuals are still learning to use computers. The growth of the systems-integration business and other services reflects some of the difficulties users have experienced. Taking advantage of distributed computing requires "thinking outside the box and beyond the obvious solutions," Price Waterhouse's Turner observed. New, more productive ways of doing business—perhaps revolutionary, when compared with the mechanized approaches to computing so common today—are likely to result. Indeed, computers and their convergence with telecommunications equipment and other technologies present the opportunity to create new businesses and even new industries.

In education, the arts, and virtually every other field of endeavor, computers and software are extensions not only of human abilities, but also of the human imagination. This is a "world of restless technology," said Yale's Perlis, and the computer is likely to insinuate itself into most societal and economic affairs. No one, he added, can "predict with any accuracy whatsoever what the role of the computer will be in our lives or our children's lives. . . . One thing we can very well be sure of is [that] it will be far different from what it is today."

Although the United States does not have a monopoly on new ideas, it is a prodigious source, demonstrated best perhaps by the pioneering innovations that launched the Computer Revolution and the Information Age. A healthy computer sector—one that does not rely on imported hardware and software—will be critical to generating and applying the new ideas that set the stage for future technological and economic advances. A computer sector that is healthier than the one that now exists will be essential for U.S. firms and the nation as a whole.

SETTING A COURSE FOR IMPROVEMENT

Colloquium participants expressed general agreement on where remedial actions are needed, differing principally on how to resolve issues in the area of standardization. They were unanimous about the need for action; as Ferguson put it, "The time is fast approaching, I think, when we really have to mobilize." The agenda emerging from the colloquium includes the following key areas requiring action.

Cooperation

Signs that the computer sector has begun to mobilize are appearing. Most striking, perhaps, is the effort to establish U.S. Memories, Inc., a joint DRAM-manufacturing facility funded by hardware industry firms that was announced in June of 1989. The production facility, if successfully launched, would work closely with SEMATECH, the privately supported and government-funded consortium that is developing methods and equipment for manufacturing advanced integrated circuits. Such novel cooperative arrangements represent a fundamental break from past ways of doing business, but more are likely to be needed, many colloquium participants believed: "We are learning about cooperation," Ferguson noted, "but Japanese firms understand it already."

Teece, of the University of California, also noted the importance of cooperation and in his writings has stressed the need to form alliances in accordance with shifting corporate and market boundaries. As the digital technologies once used almost exclusively in computers continue to spread to telecommunications, consumer electronics, and other areas, new interfirm relationships will be required to harness the manufacturing, marketing, and other capabilities required to compete in global markets.

The Role of Government

"We need government support," said Heller of EDS, "but let me also point out that we need to support the government." The nature of this now-essential relationship, which also includes universities, has been slow to materialize. A major obstacle is the fragmented structure of the federal government and industry.

Given the environment in which computer-related industries operate, what does the computer sector need from government? According to several computer sector representatives, the answer is likely to involve creating conditions that help businesses and government to adjust to competition in a global economy. "Whether we succeed or fail," said John Doyle of Hewlett Packard, "depends on how we manage our businesses and how the government manages the business environment."

Most colloquium participants saw the government as playing an enabling role, as setting up a policy and regulatory framework that accommodates the flexibility needed to compete in global markets and fosters a long-term strategic view of competitive issues.

Taking this argument further, Paul Turner, director of research at Price Waterhouse Technology Center, cautioned against an active, protectionist posture. "Like it or not," he pointed out, "we are now part of a global economy with complex interdependencies that are ill understood. In such circumstances it is surely wise to recall the obligation of physician to patient expressed by Hippocrates: 'First do no harm.'"

In areas such as education and tax and trade policy, all of which are vitally important to the computer sector, the government must play a lead role. According to many participants, that leadership responsibility should also extend to initiatives designed to create an infrastructure for the Information Age, including a national computer network. With the aid of industry, government should be addressing what infrastructural elements are needed and determining which elements are likely to emerge through the marketplace and which will require federal or state incentives, Teece advised.

Responsibility for other initiatives deemed critical to the performance of the computer sector, Teece also recommended, should rest with private industry, assisted at times by government. "If there should be an industrial policy," he said, "it should be what I call a private industrial policy, led by industry, with industry dollars, perhaps supplemented by a small amount of government dollars."

Manufacturing

Speaker after speaker emphasized the importance of competence in manufacturing, reinforcing the conclusions reached in many examinations of the nation's competitiveness. It is an acknowledged fact that foreign competitors that have eclipsed U.S. firms in many domestic and international markets have achieved their market-leading positions on the strength of their manufacturing capabilities. The ability of the hardware firms to recover market share and to fend off challenges in product areas they still dominate will be determined largely by their ability to make high-quality products efficiently and to insert innovations quickly into their product designs and manufacturing processes.

"The primary ingredient for success in the next decade," said IBM's Toole, "is speed—speed in development and speed in delivering derivative products of very high quality to the marketplace. To win, one needs to be competitive in all areas—competitive designs; well-trained employees; a strong infrastructure of tools, materials, and components; and much-improved manufacturing prowess."

Unfortunately, the means to upgrade manufacturing capabilities in the computer sector are diminishing. "The first problem that we face collectively," Ferguson maintained, "[is the declining capabilities in a] number of base technologies, component technologies, and component markets [that] are quite critical to the ability of a downstream systems firm to succeed in the computer industry."

Standards

Perhaps the most contentious issue discussed at the colloquium, standardization is gaining international momentum, and the U.S. computer sector must reckon with it. One way to view standards was characterized by Teece. "The whole role of standards is one that cannot be underestimated," he said, "because control of standards confers protections akin to patents."

The discussion about standards should not revolve around whether there should be standards or not, according to Teece. "The point to recognize is that if one controls standards, one can turn that into a competitive advantage." Morris and others noted that the standards game is international and that "universal international" standards can place U.S. vendors at a disadvantage. Consequently, harmonizing the actions of all U.S. parties—individual firms, the computer sector, and the government—is necessary.

The challenge may be even greater than the colloquium's discussion of technical aspects suggests. The United States is in some sense outnumbered in international standards arenas, because each country effectively has an equal vote. Consequently, innovations, leadership, and early deployment in this country can be vitiated by politics. The current one-country/one-vote system could be used by regions to protect local businesses by promoting a series of mutually incompatible standards adopted in individual regions, although this would ultimately be to the disadvantage of all involved, given the benefits of standardization discussed elsewhere in this report.

Education

Concerns about education ranged from the sector's needs for people with scientific and engineering talent to the broader need for education to support more and better uses of computer-related technologies. The government has traditionally been crucial in providing support for the education of the country's computer scientists and engineers. The results have been extremely positive, according to Stardent's Bell, who maintained, "I think we [the United States] have the most creative engineers. I think we have the finest scientists in computer science going." However, in comparison to the level of effort other countries are now expending, he said, "we do have a training problem."

The nation cannot afford to carry the burden of 25 percent of its high-school-age youth dropping out, according to Heller, who argued that there is a mismatch between education and other institutions that compose our economic infrastructure and the evolving economy: "Most of the institutions of the U.S. infrastructure were created to administer the Industrial Age society" and may now be in some respects obsolete.

Obviously, the interests of the computer sector are affected by this national problem. "For marketing to succeed," Perlis said, "there has to be a market. . . . Not only do we need an educated work force to be able to perform jobs, but we need an educated force that wants to know [and is] interested in essentially expanding [its] own knowledge." In the not-so-distant-future, in Perlis' view, computers and their applications will be integral to virtually every effort intended to extend one's personal knowledge.

Widespread and imaginative use of computers in education can help to better equip tomorrow's adults for contributing to U.S. society, several participants suggested. In turn, new, more effective uses of computers may evolve from the familiarity with the technology that is cultivated through education and training. The future industrial competitiveness of the entire nation, one speaker noted, may largely be determined by how effectively the general population uses computers.

CLOSING OBSERVATIONS

The agenda that emerges from the colloquium implies the need for sustained follow-up measures by industry, government, and universities, acting together and independently. The nature of the necessary interaction, as well as the mechanisms and the extent of cooperation, must be defined through a continuing dialogue that has only just begun. From this dialogue, perhaps, will come the necessary leadership to ensure that the United States responds effectively to the strategic challenges mounted by foreign competitors. Fragmented, piecemeal responses will not be sufficient. One clear lesson of the 1980s is that simply invoking the need for leadership is not enough. For government and industry, incremental tinkering at the margin will not be enough, either. The Computer Science and Technology Board will examine several of the issues raised in this colloquium in more detail, and it urges decisionmakers in industry, government, and academia to do so as well.

APPENDIXES

Appendix A
Colloquium Program

Monday, May 22, 1989

8:00 p.m. **Keynote Address**

 Clyde V. Prestowitz, Jr., Senior Associate,
  Carnegie Endowment

Tuesday, May 23, 1989

8:30 a.m. **Introduction and Welcome**

 Robert M. White, President,
  National Academy of Engineering
 Samuel H. Fuller (Colloquium Chairman),
  Vice President of Research, Digital Equipment Corporation

8:45 a.m. **Hardware Panel**

Chair: **Robert W. Lucky**, Executive Director, Research Communications
  Sciences Division, AT&T Bell Laboratories
 C. Gordon Bell, Vice President, Research and Development,
  Ardent Computer Corporation*
 Charles H. Ferguson, Postdoctoral Associate, Center for
  Technology Policy and Industrial Development,
  Massachusetts Institute of Technology

---

* Ardent has since merged with Stellar Computer to become Stardent Computer, Inc.

Gordon E. Moore, Chairman,
 Intel Corporation
Patrick A. Toole, Senior Vice President and General Manager of
 Technology Products, IBM Corporation

10:15 a.m. **Break**

10:30 a.m. **Software Panel**

Chair: **Samuel H. Fuller**, Vice President of Research, Digital Equipment
             Corporation
            Laszlo A. Belady, Vice President and Program Director,
             Microelectronics and Computer Technology Corporation
            James H. Morris, Professor of Computer Science, Carnegie
             Mellon University
            Alan J. Perlis, Professor of Computer Science, Yale University
            Lawrence G. Tesler, Vice President of Advanced Technologies,
             Apple Computer, Inc.

12:00 p.m. **Lunch in the Refectory Alcove**

1:00 p.m.   **Services and Systems Integration Panel**

Chair: **Irving Wladawsky-Berger**, Vice President, Data Systems Division
             and General Manager Kingston, IBM Corporation
            Jeffrey M. Heller, Senior Vice President, Electronic Data Systems
            Paul A. Turner, Director of Research, Price Waterhouse
             Technology Center
            Sam R. Willcoxon, President of Business Market Group, AT&T

2:30 p.m.   **Break**

2:45 p.m.   **Marketing and Business Aspects Panel**

Chair: **William J. Spencer**, Vice President, Corporate Research Group,
             Xerox Corporation
            John L. Doyle, Executive Vice President, Hewlett Packard
             Company
            William R. Hambrecht, President, Hambrecht & Quist
            Richard S. Rosenbloom, Professor, Graduate School of Business
             Administration, Harvard University
            David J. Teece, Professor, W. A. Haas School of Business,
             University of California at Berkeley

4:15 p.m.   **Synthesis, Recommendations, and Response**

Appendix B
Colloquium Participants

Norman Achilles, U.S. Department of State
Donald M. Austin, U.S. Department of Energy
David Beck, U.S. International Trade Commission
Laszlo A. Belady, Microelectronics and Computer Technology Corporation
Brian C. Belanger, U.S. Department of Commerce
C. Gordon Bell, Stardent Computer, Inc.
Kathleen C. Bernard, Cray Research, Inc.
Joel Birnbaum, Hewlett Packard Company
Jane Bortnick, Library of Congress
Michael Boudin, U.S. Department of Justice
Charles Brownstein, National Science Foundation
James H. Burrows, U.S. Department of Commerce
Virginia Castor, U.S. Department of Defense
Skip Dalton, Digital Equipment Corporation
Ambassador Peter Jon de Vos, U.S. Department of State
John L. Doyle, Hewlett Packard Company
C. F. Emde, National Aeronautics and Space Administration
Charles H. Ferguson, Massachusetts Institute of Technology
Samuel H. Fuller, Digital Equipment Corporation
Oliver Grave, Federal Trade Commission
Bruce Guile, National Academy of Engineering
William R. Hambrecht, Hambrecht & Quist
Christopher H. Hankin, U.S. Department of State
Jeffrey M. Heller, Electronic Data Systems

Lee Holcomb, National Aeronautics and Space Administration
Kenwin Jarboe, Senate Subcommittee on Government Information and
    Regulation
Raymond L. Jones, U.S. Department of Commerce
Robert E. Kahn, Corporation for National Research Initiatives
Philip Kardis, Senate Committee on Budget
William M. Kendall-Johnston, U.S. Department of State
V. N. Kryuvov, Embassy of the U.S.S.R.
Alfred M. Lee, U.S. Department of Commerce
Robert W. Lucky, AT&T Bell Laboratories
William Maher, Federal Communications Commission
John E. McPhee, U.S. Department of Commerce
Samuel Merrill, Jr., Library of Congress
George P. Millburn, U.S. Department of Defense
Katie Miller, Senate Judiciary Committee
Gordon E. Moore, Intel Corporation
James H. Morris, Carnegie Mellon University
James M. Murphy, Jr., Office of the U.S. Trade Representative
David B. Nelson, U.S. Department of Energy
Michael R. Nelson, Senate Committee on Commerce, Science and
    Transportation
James D. Otis, Supercomputer Systems, Inc.
Charles T. Owens, National Science Foundation
Abraham Peled, IBM T.J. Watson Research Center
Jorge Perez-Lopez, U.S. Department of Labor
Alan J. Perlis, Yale University
N. Scott Phillips, House Armed Services Committee
James R. Porter, National Academy of Engineering
Clyde V. Prestowitz, Jr., Carnegie Endowment
J. Mark Pullen, Defense Advanced Research Projects Agency
Raj Reddy, Carnegie Mellon University
William A. Reinsch, Office of Senator John Heinz
Cesare Rosati, U.S. Department of State
Richard S. Rosenbloom, Harvard University
Gary Russell, U.S. Department of Labor
Steven Saboe, U.S. Department of State
Liz Sadove, House Committee on Energy and Commerce
William Scherlis, Defense Advanced Research Projects Agency
Jacob Schwartz, Defense Advanced Research Projects Agency
Mary Shaw, Carnegie Mellon University
Michael Skarzynsky, U.S. Department of Commerce
V. Slavyantsev, Embassy of the U.S.S.R.
William J. Spencer, Xerox Corporation

Stephen L. Squires, Defense Advanced Research Projects Agency
Will Stackhouse, Jet Propulsion Laboratory
David J. Teece, University of California at Berkeley
Lawrence G. Tesler, Apple Computer, Inc.
Andre M. van Tilborg, Office of Naval Research
Patrick A. Toole, IBM Corporation
Paul A. Turner, Price Waterhouse Technology Center
Thomas A. Weber, National Science Foundation
Harvey Weiss, Digital Equipment Corporation
Ambassador E. Allan Wendt, U.S. Department of State
Robert M. White, Control Data Corporation
Robert M. White, National Academy of Engineering
Mary Wileden, U.S. Department of the Treasury
Sam R. Willcoxon, AT&T
Deborah Wince-Smith, U.S. Department of Commerce
Irving Wladawsky-Berger, IBM Corporation
William Wulf, National Science Foundation

Staff

Marjory S. Blumenthal, Executive Director
Damian M. Saccocio, Staff Officer
Margaret A. Knemeyer, Staff Associate
Mark Bello, CSTB Consultant
Pamela R. Rodgers, CSTB Consultant
Donna F. Allen, Administrative Secretary
Catherine A. Sparks, Secretary